Where Have You Gone, Starlight Cafe?

On U. S. Highways 77 and 166

"It was a family business. The wives and children all worked. Sometimes we children would grumble and wish our folks were not in 'that' business. But we all look back with fond memories of the local customers who were also friends and neighbors, and also all the wonderful people who worked with us in the restaurant, too."

Patricia Gochis Stigers, in discussing her family's former Purity Cafe, Arkansas City, Kansas

America's Golden Era Roadside Restaurants

Where Have You Gone, Starlight Cafe?

by Will Anderson

Anderson & Sons' Publishing Co.
7 Bramhall Terrace
Portland, Maine 04103

Other Roadside Books By The Author

New England Roadside Delights (1989)
Mid-Atlantic Roadside Delights (1991)
Good Old Maine (1993)
More Good Old Maine (1995)

Library of Congress Catalogue Card Number 97-95027

Will Anderson 1940-
1. Popular Culture 2. Americana

ISBN 0-9601056-9-7

Studio photography by A. & J. DuBois Commercial Photography, Lewiston, Maine
Front cover design assistance by Dick Hubsch, Hubsch Studio, Carmel, New York
Typeset and printed by Spectrum Printing and Graphics, Auburn, Maine
Bound by Bay State Bindery, Boston, Massachusetts
Text Stock: 100lb. Somerset Gloss Recycled, S.D.Warren Co., Skowhegan, Maine
Cover Stock: 12pt. Kromekote, Champion International Corp., Hamilton, Ohio

Cover graphics, clockwise from upper left:

Circa 1950 postcard view, Western Cafe, Rock Springs, Wyoming
Circa 1940 postcard view, Pete's Cafe, Boonville, Missouri
Circa 1945 postcard view, Penn State Flyer, Allentown, Pennsylvania

Table of Contents

Acknowledgments

**Without the help of a lot of wonderful people WHERE HAVE YOU
GONE, STARLIGHT CAFE? would most certainly still be
somewhere back down the road. Special thanks to:**

Doug Alder, Dixie College, St. George, Utah • Agnes Arnold, Texarkana, Arkansas • Peter D. Bachelder, Ellsworth, Maine • Dean Baker, Marietta, Georgia • Kathie Barrie, Portland Public Library, Portland, Maine • Prudence Barry, Portland Public Library, Portland, Maine • George & Marie Bogas, Dubuque, Iowa • Pen Bogert, Filson Club Historical Society, Louisville, Kentucky • Edgar Boles, City of Albuquerque, Albuquerque, New Mexico • Ned P. Booher, Kokomo, Indiana • David C. Buhler, Salt Lake City, Utah • Tacie N. Campbell, Mississippi River Museum, Dubuque, Iowa • Doris Cannon, Clayton, North Carolina • Pat Chapman, Norelius Community Library, Denison, Iowa • Debbie Charpentier, Millicent Library, Fairhaven, Massachusetts • Pete Christos, St. Augustine, Florida • Annie Clark, Willimantic Public Library, Willimantic, Connecticut • Al Coleman, Norwood, Ohio • Larry Cultrera, Medford, Massachusetts • Helen Daddona, Sayre, Pennsylvania • Paul D'Aessandro, Portland Public Library, Portland, Maine • Mary Douglass, Smoky Hill Museum, Salina, Kansas • Fred L. Fearing, Elizabeth City, North Carolina • Lora Lee Freed, Mohave County Historical Society, Kingman, Arizona • Cindy Gasaway, City of Plainview, Plainview, Texas • Steven Goldberg, Portland Public Library, Portland, Maine • Carol Graf, Kokomo-Howard County Public Library, Kokomo, Indiana • Mona R. Grafton, Mattoon Public Library, Mattoon, Illinois • Georgia Greer, Jonesborough, Tennessee • J. Hurley Hagood, Hannibal, Missouri • Bill Hamel, *Journal Gazette,* Mattoon, Illinois • Fitzgerald F. Harder, Arkansas City, Kansas • John Hart, Johnson City Public Library, Johnson City, Tennessee • Marie Hays, Albuquerque, New Mexico • Peggy Hobson, Kokomo-Howard County Visitors' Bureau, Kokomo, Indiana • Alice Howell, Kearney, Nebraska • Ned Irwin, East Tennessee State University, Johnson City, Tennessee • Todd Johnson, Public Library of Johnston County & Smithfield, Smithfield, North Carolina • Eldon Kohlman, Val Verde County Historical Commission, Del Rio, Texas • Donna Landis, London, Ohio • Vickie Leverette, Waycross Tourism & Conference Bureau, Waycross, Georgia • Lee Lincoln, Whitehead Memorial Museum, Del Rio, Texas • Kim Lopiccolo, Rock Springs Library, Rock Springs, Wyoming • Guadalupe Lopez, Winslow, Arizona • Marlene Magness, The Historical Society of Harford County, Bel Air, Maryland • Joe McKenzie, Salina Public Library, Salina, Kansas • Janet Miller, Kentland, Indiana • Bob Noelke, Waterloo, Illinois • Mo Sue Palmer, Albuquerque Museum, Albuquerque, New Mexico • Elaine Parker, South Portland Public Library, South Portland, Maine • Willard Phillips, Elkins, West Virginia • Eleanor Rick, Mt. Holly, New Jersey • Ruth Ridgeway, South Windham, Connecticut • Charles Robbins, Bel Air, Maryland • Randy Roberts, Thomaston, Maine • Robert San Clemente, Days Creek, Oregon • Henry R. Schneck, Jr., Allentown, Pennsylvania • Edith Serkownek, Warren County Historical Society, Warren, Pennsylvania • George T. Shackelford, City of Texarkana, Texarkana, Texas • Ethel A. Shiffrar, Santa Maria, California • Dessie Little Simmons, Watauga Ass'n. Of Genealogists, Johnson City, Tennessee • Harold M. Slater, St. Joseph, Missouri • Patricia Gochis Stigers, Wichita, Kansas • Larry R. Stobbs, City of St. Joseph, St. Joseph, Missouri • Jerri Fielding Sullivan, City of Odessa, Odessa, Texas • Shirley Taylor, Louisville, Kentucky • Gary Thomas, Beverly, Massachusetts • Ginger and Shirley Tilicek, Schulenburg, Texas • Ron Tubertini, Mt. Holly, New Jersey • Richard S. Warner, Tulsa, Oklahoma

Preface

Once upon a time there was a family who lived in New York state. And that family loved to take auto trips. Or at least the father and son did.

That family was mine. I was the son. The time was the years 1946 to 1959. At first our mode of transportation was a wonderful big old pre-war Packard ("Ask The Man Who Owns One"), which was only fitting because my father's father had worked for Packard for something like 26 years. I yet recall the day I accompanied my father down to the Bronx, to a place where a man sold Cities Service (now Citgo) gas and used cars. My father had sold him the Packard. It was a sad day.

A succession of other cars followed: a 1950 Ford, a 1953 "Dynaflow Drive" Buick, a 1957 Ford. Regardless of make and model of car, though, one thing was for certain: that we'd be on the road for parts unknown every summer. Sometimes it was New England, sometimes upstate New York, sometimes Pennsylvania, mostly down south. Far off destinations the likes of Williamsburg, Charleston, Savannah, St. Augustine, the Great Smokies, even as far as Biloxi and Mobile and New Orleans.

Sometimes just my dad and I would go. But usually the whole family would make the trip. That meant my mother and younger sister, too. They loved to swim, but my father and I preferred the historic sights. And I don't think my father ever passed up an antique shop. He was real good at making u-turns. I used to try to work in a minor league baseball game or two. I still have 1950s' souvenir programs from the Lancaster (Pa.) Red Roses, the Augusta (Ga.) Tigers, and the Chattanooga Lookouts.

A few family snapshots from along the way.

Top to bottom: my father at the plate at Doubleday Field, Cooperstown, New York, 1952; my sister Carol and I atop Skyline Drive, Virginia, 1957; Carol and the sign for Ladd's Wayside Inn, Bethel, Maine, 1953; the whole family somewhere in the Great Smokies, 1954.

But mostly what I remember are the restaurants. Eating. That my mother would just about always change her mind about what she wanted six or so minutes after she'd ordered. You could almost set a watch by it. How my sister – regardless of what kind of restaurant we were in – would order a hamburger and chocolate ice cream. We could be in Sam's Seafood Paradise and she'd still order a hamburger. She was not very adventuresome.

We often ate "fancy" in the evening. But for breakfast and lunch it was places that served just plain old "regular" food. I liked those places the best.

And we rarely ate in any sort of a chain. My father felt strongly that part of a vacation was local color, and trying different things. He figured there wasn't much sense in driving 1,000 miles and eating in a place that was a clone of a place back home. That seemed pretty astute to me then. It still does today.

It's now four decades later. My father and my mother have, sadly, passed away. My sister is into sailing and skiing. But I still like to hit the road and see what's out there. I thought perhaps you'd like to join me.

Will Anderson

Portland, Maine
March 19, 1998

WHERE HAVE YOU GONE, STARLIGHT CAFE?
is dedicated to a pair of very special people:

**My wife and partner, Catherine Buotte, for
her encouragement, proofreading extraordinaire,
and "co-adventuring" our trip across America and back**

and

**My friend and buddy, Tom Hug, for allowing me
free and full access to his truly marvelous collection
of advertising Americana, as well as encouragement
and support.**

Introduction: A Short History Of Roadside Fare

Before there could be the Golden Era of roadside restaurants there had to be a beginning. And it was humble. Early motorists – more often called "autoists" or "automobilists" – were a hardy lot who strayed beyond their town or city corporate limits at some considerable peril. Vehicles were primitive. Roads were horrendous. Services were worse.

As U.S. motor vehicle sales multiplied, though, things could not help but change. Automobile registrations shot up six-fold – from a total of 77,400 to a total of 458,300 – in the five-year period between 1905 and 1910. *That* prompted American business to take notice.

As Maine Goes

The State of Maine, although far and away the largest of the six New England states, doesn't really amount to a row of beans – baked or otherwise – when it comes to overall U.S. land mass or population. Still, it's long been considered a barometer of what's to come. "As Maine goes, so goes the nation" is an old saying that's probably more true than untrue. (Ed. note: in addition, residing in Maine has allowed me the opportunity to undertake a pretty substantial amount of research on early Maine motoring.). So…here's what happened in Maine (and, most likely, the rest of America as well) with respect to getting a bite to eat while out on the road.

In 1909 there began to appear ads aimed at the autoist. Ye Surf House, located on the strand in Old Orchard Beach (a resort town 15 miles south of Portland), was a pioneer. The inn's ads in the Portland *Evening Express* in early July stated – in a paragraph all its own, no less – "We solicit automobile and banquet parties." (with an "automobile party" being a group of people traveling together by auto). "Best of service to automobilists" promised the Hillcroft Inn, in York Harbor, in talking up their lobster and chicken dinners, while the noted Bangor House, in Bangor, rang out "Special Attention Given Automobile Tourists."

By 1913 establishments were going one step further: instead of merely saying, in effect, "We're here *if* you're hungry and you need us," they began to suggest themselves as a *reason* for a spin in the motor car. A prime example is the ad placed, again in the Portland *Evening Express*, issue of July 2nd, by the Merriconeag Inn, in South Harpswell, for its Shore Dinners. The ad's tag line, "Finest Auto Trip out of Portland," does more than invite one to stop in if one happens to be in the neighborhood. It says instead: "Come on up, the food's fine." (Ed. note: a shore dinner, an old New England summer tradition, generally consists of a cup of fish chowder, lobster, steamed clams, corn on the cob, a roll or blueberry muffin, and a slice of pie. It is not a light meal!).

"Square Deal Asked"

The Merriconeag and its companions, however, were most likely far from the norm. An article, entitled "Square Deal Asked By Motor Tourists," in the June 29, 1913 issue of the *Portland Sunday Telegram*, makes the point that oft times the "special attention" given to motorists was to overcharge them. To be "charged a tariff and a half" as a result of arriving "in duster and goggles," as the article phrased it. Nor was the quality of what was offered given very high marks, either. Too much emphasis on quantity of choice rather than quality of basics was the writer's major complaint. Wrote he, with a helping of mirth thrown in: "The tourist will in 90 percent of the cases care more that the eggs and vegetables served be strictly fresh than that a choice of fancy salads is offered or that three varieties of oysters of doubtful birthplace head the menu."

What the motorist clearly needed was a place of his/her own. It would happen. But it would take awhile.

The Roaring Twenties

It was not until the early 1920s, in Vacationland at least, that there was much of a change with respect to roadside offerings. The year 1921 saw an explosion in "Auto Parties" advertisements. "Motor out and have a REAL BROILED CHICKEN DINNER with fresh vegetables," proclaimed the Hillcrest Lodge (on Sebago Lake). "A journey by auto over the Ossipee Trail (Ed. note: early motor routes were often referred to as "Trails.") brings you to this delightful spot," boasted the

Dyke Mountain Farm Inn (also in Sebago, roughly 45 miles from Portland). "When Motoring Through Freeport Stop for a Shore Dinner" was the contribution of the Elm Tree Inn (located, not surprisingly, in Freeport, about 12 miles north of Portland on what was then called the Atlantic Highway and is now called U.S. Route 1). Then there was "When you are out auto riding call at Fickett's and try our Lobster and Chicken Dinners," from Fickett's Inn (in South Orrington, a dozen miles south of Bangor).

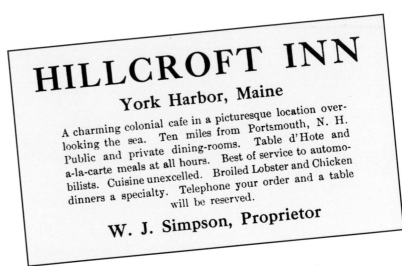

"Best of service to automobilists." Ad, summer of 1909. Some businesspeople, at least, were beginning to see the light: that "automobilists" were here to stay and that providing services for them was going to be BIG business.

There were more. Many more. But all, seemingly, were still the work of been-around-a-spell establishments now aiming their plates at motorists.

In 1922-1923, however, there finally began to appear real live establishments created specifically for real live auto travelers. Most were far from elegant. An article bylined Eastport (which lives up to its name: located about 100 miles due east of Bangor, it is the easternmost city in the United States) in the May 22, 1923 issue of the *Bangor Daily News* portrayed one such establishment, eight miles outside of Eastport, that had sprung up the year before. Its size was given as 16' x 18' and, sure enough, there's a photo that shows a small, wood-frame, shingled structure with a hip roof. Also included in the photo are the proud proprietors, Mr. and Mrs. George W. Talbot, along with their young daughter. The article, entitled "Roadside Tea-Rooms are in Bud," stated that Mr. Talbot was a successful farmer who added to his family's income via his "tea room." He was far from alone. In the May 13th issue of the *Portland Sunday Telegram* the head of the Maine Publicity Bureau told as how he'd recently asked a Maine farmer what he lived on. The reply: " 'Taters in the winter and tourists in the summer." Concurred the Eastport article, "Farmers' families are now giving more attention to refreshment stands erected near their farms and within the month these unique shops have been opened for the auto season running to late November." Continued the write-up: "Not only is ice cream, fresh from the farms, provided to auto parties, but home cooked foods, fruit, buttermilk, and quick lunches are now on the menu." The article concluded: "With food for the hungry, drink for the thirsty, and rest for the weary,

there is now more pleasure for auto parties going into the country."

Less than six weeks later, on July 1st, a similar article appeared in the *Portland Sunday Telegram*. Headlined "Autoists Tarry At Wayside Tea Room, Top O' The Hill," the author told the tale of a Mrs. Evelyn Ward who had just opened a tea room near her home in North Windham (20 miles northwest of Portland). Although not a farmer, Mrs. Ward's intention was the same as Mr. and Mrs. Talbot's: to satisfy the hunger of the motoring public and to profit by so doing. Phrased the article: "She has attractively fitted up a small building bearing this designation (the Top O' The Hill), where automobile parties can be accommodated with an appetizing variety of food."

So it would appear that the "tea room" – a term often used as a catchall for any "homespun" enterprise where meals were served – was the first in line. The first to stand up and say "Hey, Mr. and Mrs. Motorist, we've come into the picture to serve you and your taste buds. Enjoy." As they prospered and grew in size and scope, others followed. Some were even so bold as to lead with "Auto" in their name. The Auto Stop Inn ("Shore And Chicken Dinners At All Hours") in Boothbay Harbor, and the Auto Rest Inn ("All Home Cooking"), in South Portland, were early Maine examples of the latter. Both were opened in the early 1920s.

As tea rooms – and "Auto Inns" – faded from view in the early 1930s a new phenomenon appeared...

Please turn to page 16

The Diner

The diner's beginnings go back to 1872. To Providence, Rhode Island, where a man by the name of Walter Scott noticed that if you wanted a square meal after sundown your only choices were the local saloon or your own kitchen.

Walter decided a remedy was in order. He took a horse-drawn wagon, cut holes on both sides, loaded up an array of sandwiches, pies, and hot coffee and stationed his wagon directly across from the *Providence Journal*. He reasoned he'd get the newspaper crews as they came off shift. But he got a lot more, too: policemen, the after-theatre crowd, just plain night owls.

Walter's success did not go unnoticed: by the early 1880s there were thirty such dining cars in operation in Providence alone.

While it was Providence that gave birth to the diner, it was Worcester, Massachusetts that brought it to far greater heights. First came Sam Jones: he took Walter Scott's idea and enlarged upon it, creating a wagon – in 1887 – spacious enough for patrons to come inside rather than having to wait outside. Next came another Worcesterite, Charles Palmer, who visualized the lunch cart's success beyond the confines of New England. He began a lunch wagon manufacturing company. That was in 1891. Yet another Worcesterite, one Thomas H. Buckley, went a step farther by not only producing, but mass producing, lunch wagons, churning out hundreds of them in the 1890s and into the better part of the first decade of this century. And last, another firm, the Worcester Lunch Car Company, became one of the nation's pre-eminent diner manufacturers, beginning in 1906 and continuing on through 1962.

New Jersey would later become the hub of the diner manufacturing world. And, as Walter Scott's creation became more and more streamlined, the term "lunch cart/wagon" gave way, in the 1920s, to "diner," a result of the structure's resemblance to the railway dining car. By any name, however, diners are as American as a big slice of apple pie...and as joyful a sight to behold.

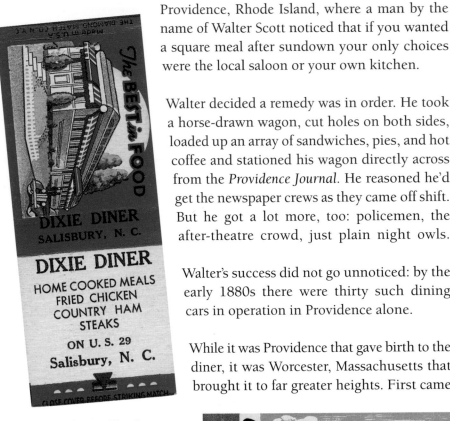

Old matchbook covers aren't as attractive as old postcards...but they sometimes come close. Here, and on the facing page, are three I'm especially fond of. All three date from 1950 or so.

The Drive-In

The Pig Stand, opened in September 1921 on the Dallas–Fort Worth Highway in Texas, is generally considered to be the world's initial drive-in restaurant. But the actual honor of first serving customers outside a restaurant, as relayed by Jim Heiman in his 1996 book, CAR HOPS AND CURB SERVICE, goes to a Harold Fortune in Memphis in 1905. Mr. Fortune managed the soda fountain in a local drug store. One especially busy evening he allowed some of his gentlemen patrons to bring their orders outside to their waiting lady friends rather than having to contend with the cramped quarters inside. The idea caught on, and it wasn't long before Fortune was engaging runners to take orders curbside and then deliver the food likewise.

The Pig Stand, however, is credited with being the first restaurant *specifically set up* to serve customers in their cars. The idea was the brainchild of Dallas candy and tobacco wholesaler J.G. Kirby – who once reputedly commented that "People with cars are so lazy that they don't want to get out of them to eat." – and well-to-do physician Dr. R.W. Jackson.

The Pig Stand was a success right from the start. A barbequed pork sandwich – the restaurant's namesake and specialty – savored in the comfort of one's own car was tough to beat. Within little more than a decade there were over sixty Pig Stands serving customers in seven states. Competitors, too, joined the drive-in ranks. Restaurant and hotel veteran Roy W. Allen teamed with Frank Wright in 1922 to open a trio of root beer stands – called, of course, A & W – in Houston. The next year Allen and Wright went a step farther and opened an A & W *Drive-In* in Sacramento. By 1933 there were 171 A & W stands and drive-ins spread across America. Hot Shoppes, begun by J.

Willard Marriott in Washington, D.C. in 1927, was another successful early drive-in chain. There were others. Amazingly, most remained successful during the Great Depression. In fact, the drive-in's greatest moment of glory may well have come when *Life* magazine pictured comely car hop Josephine Powell of Houston, wonderfully attired in what would otherwise have passed for a majorette's outfit, smack dab on the front cover of its issue of February 26, 1940.

Lights on for service.

a phenomenon that has come to dominate American roadside eating. That phenomenon was – and is – the chain/franchise.

Unchained Melody

Chains are actually not that new. A man by the name of Fred Harvey saw to that. An English immigrant who began life in America as a dishwasher, Harvey moved up the restaurant ladder until, in 1859, he became co-proprietor of a restaurant in St. Louis. From there he went on to form a string of Harvey Houses across the western states and territories that numbered a solid 45 at the time of his demise in 1901.

Other early chains included James A. Whitcomb and his Baltimore Dairy Lunch (100-plus units in operation

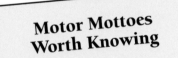

Motor Mottoes Worth Knowing

Still motors run sweet.

Where there's gas there's hope.

Fools pass on hills and curves.

A wise driver maketh a glad auto.

It is better to be slow than sorry.

Where ther's a nail there's a puncture.

To speed is human; to get caught a fine.

From the Motoring Section,
Portland Sunday Telegram,
July 10, 1923

by the early 1920s), Child's (over 80 units by 1920), Thompson's Restaurants (100-plus outlets by 1915), Waldorf Lunch (75 units by 1920), the White Castle and White Tower hamburger chains ("Buy 'em by the sack"), Howard Johnson's, etc., etc.

And, yes, chains do have their place. They insure uniformity and that can be ok. It certainly does seem, though, as if uniformity has gotten out of hand. Uniformity has turned to blandness. To the point where virtually every "strip" in America consists of the very same cookie cutter cast of characters: McDonald's, Burger King, Wendy's, Arby's, Big Boy, Taco Bell, KFC, Pizza Hut, etc., etc., etc. You know who they are.

No such suspects appear in WHERE HAVE YOU GONE, STARLIGHT CAFE? Nope, these are the real McCoy. With mom and dad (and probably the kids, too) on the scene. With the French fries prepared by hand right there, not 1,100 or so miles away. Ditto the hamburgers and cheeseburgers. Was the food any better in the real McCoy? Maybe yes. Maybe no. Maybe so. Ah, but was the visual variety and beauty – what our eyes and our imaginations gazed upon as we motored along America's roadways – any better?

You bet it was!

What to wear when out for a spin. As Maine goes...

Ad, *Venture*, the literary magazine of Hallowell High School, Hallowell, Maine, April, 1925

Part 1: The Top 40

WHERE HAVE YOU GONE, STARLIGHT CAFE? is the result of curiosity. I have collected roadside (i.e. cabin court/motel, filling station/garage, restaurant, etc.) postcards for years. As I've grown older I've found myself wondering whatever happened to all those places pictured on all those postcards. I finally decided to select a "top 40" from the category that intrigued me the most – restaurants – and find out what *did* happen to them.

I thought, also, that via the selected 40 I would most likely end up with a pretty good idea of what happened to all of the other great places that were out there in that Golden Era of roadside architecture, 1930–1960, as well. The 40 would serve, if you will, as a pretty solid representative sampling.

What did I look for in selecting the top 40? It's difficult to say, but visual appeal, geographical and small town/big town diversity, and warmth (that "Welcome, come on in" persona) all played a role. That established, my wife Catherine and I set out – by way of both correspondence and in-person visits – to try to capture the "life story" of each of the 40. These stories, accompanied by the postcard views (each of which is enlarged by 40% for additional viewing pleasure) that inspired us in the first place, grace the next four-score pages.

One additional note: although there have probably been a goodly number of eateries actually named "Starlight Cafe," there are none, alas, included in WHERE HAVE YOU GONE, STARLIGHT CAFE? It's a name that, somehow, just felt right.

Come on along…

Baker's Cafe
Routes 59, 60, 66, and 69
Afton, Oklahoma

Afton, which sits about 80 miles northeast of Tulsa, has never been a big town. But it used to be bigger than it is now. "It was pretty booming then (in the 1940s and 1950s)," recounts lifelong resident Martha Giles. "We used to have a railroad and a Roadway Express terminal. Things were pretty busy."

Part of those busy days was Baker's Cafe. Located on Main Street, which also happened to be the legendary Route 66 (as well as three other routes), Baker's went back to 1931. In that year the husband and wife team of Clinton and Lillie Baker purchased a small restaurant on highways 59, 60, 66, and 69 in downtown Afton. Recalls Clinton and Lillie's son Dean: "The Frisco Railroad terminal was behind the cafe and there were four highways in front. It was a busy place."

During World War II, Baker's, by then enlarged to seat 120, was especially busy. Recalls Dean Baker again: "Dad worked 16 hours a day during the war when my older brother Jack was in the service. So did all the rest of the family, too. Troop trains would pull up to the depot and dad would feed the whole train. Local people ate there, too, usually on Saturdays and Sundays. Fried chicken ('southern fried, of course!') and good Folger's coffee were the keys to success."

Another key was hard work. Clinton tasted everything that came out of the kitchen. If it wasn't right he threw it out. He was especially proud of the cafe's breads and desserts, and the pastry chef would routinely turn out 40–50 pies as well as biscuits, doughnuts, and sweet rolls every day, eight hours a day, seven days a week.

Clinton Baker was known for his good heart as well as his food. He created a room behind the cafe where the truck drivers and railroad crews could read or play dominoes during their layovers. And during the Depression he'd never turn a hungry person away. For an hour's work Clinton would feed anyone and everyone and then give them 50¢ to boot.

In 1947 Dean's twin brother Gene was seriously hurt in an automobile accident, and Clinton and Lillie sold the restaurant in order to care for their son. The building continued to be operated as a restaurant into the 1960s. It is now home to the Happiness Is daycare center. (Ed. note: for more on the building today please see page 112.).

FAMOUS FOR STEAKS AND CHICKEN DINNERS

BAKER'S CAFE, Afton, Okla.

50 Miles West of Joplin and 80 Miles East of Tulsa on U. S. Hiways 66 and 69

Circa 1945 Postcard View

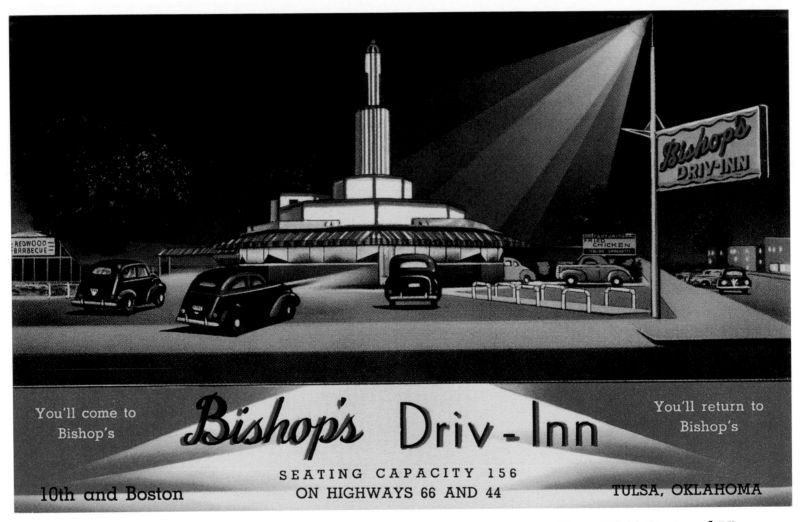

Circa 1940 Postcard View

Bishop's Driv-Inn
10th St. & Boston Ave./Routes 44 & 66
Tulsa, Oklahoma

The Bishop Driv-Inn's slogan was "Where Southern hospitality has met culinary art." It was to be a short-lived meeting: the Driv-Inn lasted but five years.

What became Bishop's Driv-Inn began as Bishop's Sandwich Shop in 1936. Its creator was William Wallace Bishop, a restaurant veteran if ever there were one. Bishop opened his first eatery in Drumright, Oklahoma in 1910; moved to Tulsa in 1915 and operated several restaurants there; later owned establishments in Oklahoma City, Dallas, Amarillo, and Hollywood.

But Bishop's 10th and Boston operation in Tulsa never quite made it. He turned it from a sandwich shop into the Driv-Inn in 1938. And it's as the Driv-Inn that it's still recalled by at least some folks in and around Tulsa. Seventy-three year old Prier

Price III remembers Bishop's as "quite a place." He especially admired the Driv-Inn's Brown Derby, a meatloaf sandwich smothered in sauce and onions. Other Prier favorites were the "real good malts" and the sirloin steak dinner for two ("for about $1.50"). Prier also remembers, somewhat less fondly, the evening he blew two tires on his father's car (a 1939 Chevrolet) by driving too fast over the curb on his way into the Driv-Inn's parking lot.

The Driv-Inn's malted milkshakes are also well recalled by Betty and Harley "Doc" Samuels, aged 73 and 78, respectively. Betty describes the malts as "real thick and chunky." She liked the hamburgers and barbeque sandwiches, too. Most of all, though, she likes it that Harley proposed to her on a date at the Driv-Inn. That was in February of 1941. They were married

seven months later. "It was a good move," Betty says unabashedly. "We're still married and we're still happy."

Chunky malts and wonderful sirloin steaks or not, however, Bishop's Driv-Inn went out of business in 1942. Local historian Richard S. Warner is of the mind that the Driv-Inn, being on Route 66, was most likely heavily dependent on passing motorists, and when the War went into full swing there just weren't many motorists doing any passing. I think Richard is right.

The building that was Bishop's Driv-Inn later served as a bus station, as the office for a used car lot, and, in the 1950s, as a drive-in restaurant again. It has long since been demolished. Its site is now cleared and is utilized as a parking lot by Tulsa Junior College.

Bridge Diner
6 Popes Island/U.S. Route 6
New Bedford, Massachusetts

Just calling a structure a "diner" doesn't make it one. To be a real diner, by diner purist standards, a diner must have been manufactured by one of the twenty or so diner-manufacturing companies that have been in business through the years, and then transported to its site. The Bridge Diner is a real diner. So, in our Top 40, are the Hopkins, Madison, Penn State Flyer, and Windham Grill. All are in the northeast, the stronghold of the diner. The White Rose, as attractive as it is, is not a real diner.

Back to the Bridge, opened in 1935 with a man named Antoine Viau as proprietor. The diner's site, on Popes Island in Acushnet Bay between New Bedford and Fairhaven, was a logical choice…directly on U.S. Route 6 heading toward Cape Cod, and home to a restaurant of one sort or another for the better part of the previous decade.

Viau passed away in 1939, and one Olaf Anderson took over as proprietor. Olaf shut down both the diner and its adjoining sea grill for a time in mid-1940: he'd decided a complete overhaul was in order. When he reopened, in early October, he ran ads that shouted "Yes, Sir! From the gleaming white walls outside to the new porcelain walls inside, it's BRAND NEW." And in case the newness didn't impress, the ads also ballyhooed a Roast Turkey Dinner ("with all the fixings") for 50¢ and luncheon specials that started at 35¢. (Ed. note: Sometime, just for the fun of it, see what you can get for 35¢ today!).

It isn't difficult to find people who recall the Bridge. And recall it affectionately. For Mary Jane Richmond, 60, it was a place to go after dances at nearby Fairhaven High in the 1950s. "It always had good home-cooked food," states she with vigor. "It was popular because of its location right on the water," says Ed Hynes, 77. But Ed is quick to add: "Actually, though, most times people were looking at their plate rather than the view. And the food was good. It was reasonable, too, and this was during the Depression." Warner Allard, 65, recalls the Bridge mostly as a "very popular nighttime spot." That it would be packed until 2:00 AM on a Saturday night. "They'd have signs – for specials – all around the wall. And the prices were right." Plus, notes Warner, "Everything came out hot. And everything came out on time. And everything was excellent." Last is Steve Foster, 65. Steve has warm memories of walking across the Route 6 Bridge from Fairhaven with his mom and dad when he was 11 or 12, during World War II. "My father had sold our car because gas rationing had gotten so strict, and we'd walk to the diner for Sunday dinner. It was a treat to eat out." Steve has warm memories of the Bridge's French fries, too. "They had really good French fries. My mother was Irish," he laughs, "and she'd always boil or mash potatoes. So French fries were something different for me. Load 'em with ketchup and wow!"

The wows ceased in late 1969. That's when the Bridge Diner – but not the Sea Grill – was demolished to make way for a steak house. Today, that, too, has been demolished. Only the old Sea Grill structure remains standing, home to a Chinese restaurant called Tofu.

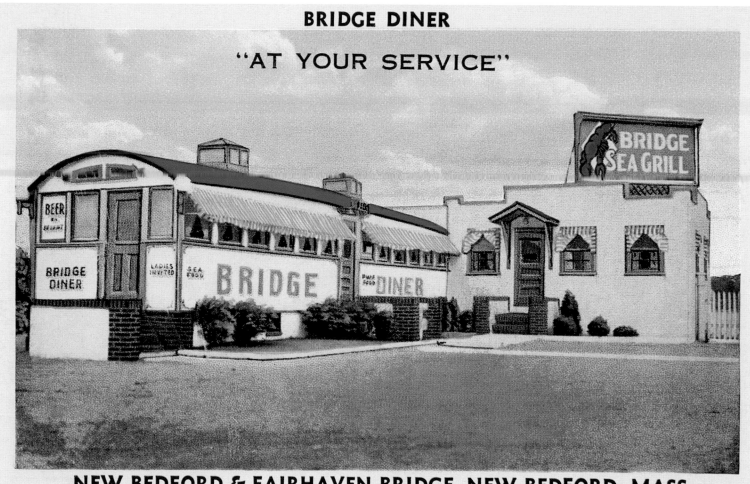

Circa 1945 Postcard View

CASA LINDA CAFE — KINGMAN, ARIZONA

Circa 1950 Postcard View

Casa Linda Cafe
505 East Front St./Route 66
Kingman, Arizona

Kingman claims to be "The Heart of Historic Route 66," the well-heralded highway that made its way from Chicago to Los Angeles. And part of Kingman's claim belonged – for over 30 years – to the Casa Linda Cafe.

The Casa Linda was started in early 1933 as the Clara Boyd Cafe; Clara Boyd, proprietor. Sundays dinners were the specialty, with ads promising "Many Courses to Choose From." Later the same year, Clara, who'd waitressed as a Harvey Girl in the then well-known Harvey House chain, decided a name change was in order. She and her husband Jimmy offered a brand new Silex Coffee Maker to the person or persons who could come up with the best suggestion. The winner was one Walter "Tuffy" Spaw, who came forth with, as you may have guessed, Casa Linda ("Beautiful House") Cafe.

But Clara and Jimmy did more than just change their restaurant's name: they also altered both the exterior and the interior. In an article in the May 6, 1933 issue of Kingman's newspaper, *The Mohave County Miner*, the Casa Linda was described as having been given "an attractive Spanish type entrance with a flagstone walk." The paper went on the report that "The main dining room has been tastefully constructed along Spanish lines, and having a seating capacity of fifty, makes a charming picture with its new oak floor, stippled walls, beamed ceiling and dark chairs and tables." The article closed by stating that "The new venture represents a considerable investment and the faith of its proprietors, Jimmy and Clara Boyd, that better times are coming for Kingman."

Little more than a year later the Boyds were at it again, adding what they named the Casa Linda Arbor. Basically an outdoor wining and dining area, it, too, was applauded by *The Miner*, as "an attractive colored cement floor, bordered with beautiful ornamental potted trees and protected overhead by rustic framework and roofing." *The Miner* closed by likening the Arbor area to "an oasis in the desert."

Clara, first with Jimmy and later with second husband Harry Quartier, carried on as owner/operator of the Casa Linda until 1959. A succession of other people then stepped in and kept the Casa Linda in business until 1964. Slogans changed, too, from "Home of Fine Foods" (1951), "Foods of Distinction" (1951-1954), "The Finest in Food" (1956), to my favorite, "Something superior for your interior!" (1963).

The longtime former restaurant is now home to a surveying firm named CSNA, short for Carlton Sons Nielson Associates. (Ed. note: for more on the building today please see page 114.).

The Court Cafe
109-111 North 4th St./Routes 66 & 85
Albuquerque, New Mexico

The Court Cafe and its successors have had an amazing longevity. The Cafe's beginnings reach back to 1925 when V.P. Katsanis, who'd previously managed the Angel Cafe at 119 North 4th Street and then the Best Ever Lunch on South 2nd Street (both in downtown Albuquerque), opened his masterpiece, the Court. He would operate it for the next twenty years and along the way he would change his name not once but twice. He dropped the "V.P." (the "V." stood for Virgil) in favor of Robert in 1927, and took Katson as his last name in 1929. By any name, though, Katsanis/Katson made the Court a true downtown hub. He then, as World War II was ending, sold the Cafe to brothers Dale, Elmer, and Harold Elliott, who continued the legacy (One of their slogans was "Where Main Highways Meet and Travelers Eat.").

Just what made the Court Cafe so special? Eighty-year-old Marie Hays, a lifelong Albuquerque resident and an aficionado almost as long, explains it well. Says Marie: "The Court Cafe was a favorite downtown gathering spot on 4th Street, just a half block north of Central Avenue (Ed. note: Central Avenue was also Route 66), then the two main streets in Albuquerque. The Court Cafe was right in the middle of it all: in the heart of the business district, one block from the Bernalillo County Courthouse, two blocks from City Hall, and two blocks from the Post Office and Federal Building.

"During the day the Court was a gathering place for a good 10¢ cup of coffee, a doughnut, and lots of good conversation. It was the haunt of politicians, businessmen, and government employees. Many a deal was made in a booth at the Court.

"The Cafe was open from early morning until late at night. The nighttime crowd was families out to dinner or people dropping in for a snack after a movie at the nearby KIMO Theatre."

Other agree with Marie. Notes octogenarian Betty Huning Hinton: "The Court was fun. I can remember when my husband came back from World War II we went downtown and the Court was the place we headed for." Arthur Loy, 83, recalls the Court as "a great place to take a date after a movie," while relative youngster Mo Sue Palmer, 54, recounts "We used to hang out there in the fifties: we'd drink coffee and smoke cigarettes, and we thought we were very sophisticated."

The Elliotts sold the Court Cafe to Roy Olguin in 1958. A year later it was sold again, to Nick Kapnison, and the name was changed to Kapnison's Court Cafe. It was later, in the seventies, the Daskalos Court Cafe. Since then the veteran eatery has had a host of other names and seen considerable physical changes as well. It is now – and has been since 1991 – the 4th Street Cafe. (Ed. note: for more on the building today please see page 111.).

**Circa 1945
Postcard View**

COURT CAFE
On Highways 66 and 85 in the heart of
ALBUQUERQUE, NEW MEXICO
Known from Coast to Coast -- 24 Hour Service
"TOURISTS COME AS YOU ARE"

5A-H610

Circa 1955 Postcard View

Cronk's Cafe
812 4th Avenue/U.S. Routes 30 & 59; Iowa Routes 4 & 141
Denison, Iowa

Denison is the home of both actress Donna Reed (born Donna Belle Mullenger in 1921) and Cronk's Cafe. And while Donna is undoubtedly more famous, Cronk's has lasted longer. Ms. Reed, unfortunately, passed away in 1986. Cronk's is still going strong.

Cronk's beginnings go back to the early 1920s when a woman known as Ma Thompson constructed a makeshift counter on the front porch of her house and sold coffee and doughnuts and the like to the truckers and travelers who passed by on the Lincoln Highway. (Ed note: the Lincoln Highway was established by the U.S. government in 1913 and was the nation's first coast-to-coast route. It was later designated U.S. Route 30.).

Circa 1927 the business, such as it was, was purchased by Lovell J. Cronk. It was

he who began the use of the name Cronk's Cafe. Then came Lovell's cousin, Claude Cronk, who ran things from the 1930s through the World War years. Lucille Waldron, now 74, recalls Claude as a heck of a guy. "During the War," she's quick to recall, "he'd pick you up and take you home. Employers don't do that now. And he'd let us eat all we wanted to, too." Continues Lucille: "Working (as a waitress) was good during the War. Soldiers were good tippers. And even during the War they (Cronk's) somehow had a good supply of steaks. When people asked me what to eat I'd recommend the butterfly filet. Sometimes I think that's why they tipped me so well...because they liked my recommendation."

Don Bartlett, 75, recalls Claude's years, too. "I used to go in there (Cronk's) as a kid. They had the best steak around, but we were kids and so we had mostly ham-

burgers and malts. They were the real malts...so thick you couldn't get them through a straw. You had to eat 'em with a spoon. One of those long spoons."

After Claude came a line-up of non-Cronk proprietors. There was Phil Russel, Tom and Doris Shaddy (who owned it when the postcard reproduced here was printed), Ev Norelius, John Skoog, and finally, Eric Skoog (John's son). Eric, who's been with the restaurant in one capacity or another since 1979, is Cronk's present proprietor. When asked why no one has ever renamed the restaurant to, say, "Shaddy's" or "Skoog's," he replies with no hesitation: "No one has ever changed the name all through the years because of the recognition it (the Cronk's name) has on the Lincoln Highway." It's a good answer. (Ed. note: for more on the Cronk's of today please see page 110.).

Dixie Restaurant
425 East Main Street
Johnson City, Tennessee

There are many success stories in WHERE HAVE YOU GONE, STARLIGHT CAFE? George Parker's story is one of them.

Born in Feri, Albania, in 1898, George Parker came to America – and Johnson City, in eastern Tennessee – in 1921. What he did from his arrival until 1930 is unknown, although it's a good bet he learned the restaurant trade by working in eateries around town. In any event, in 1930 Parker and his wife Mary opened a small sandwich shop at 425 East Main Street. They called it the Dixie Barbeque.

For over four decades the Parkers owned and operated the Dixie. They enlarged it several times, to where it seated 150. They were proud of what they created, and the slogans/statements utilized in their advertising over those four-plus decades reflect it:

"The Dixie Restaurant Is A Treasure House Of Good Food And Hospitality"

"Originators of the Most Imitated Sandwiches in the Southland"

and, from the address side of the postcard pictured here

"Today, the Dixie is one of the outstanding Restaurants in the Southland"

The Dixie is well remembered. Hunter Jackson, 72, loved the restaurant's carhop service. Even during the War (World War II) he and his friends came up with enough gas to take a spin to the Dixie. "We did a lot of doubledating," he admits. Jerry Teeter, 58, loved the hamburgers and, in the late fifties, he and his '56 Chevy (red and white, with skirts) could often be found at 425 East Main. Another fan of the Dixie's hamburgers was Dessie Little Simmons. Now 81, Dessie recalls the 1930s and that the Dixie's hamburgers were "huge, about the size of the bottom of a plate. I haven't had as good a one since," she adds. Last is Chris Rhyne, 41, who remembers going to the Dixie with his granddad, Harlin. "When I was a kid, back in 1961 or so, I'd go there (the Dixie) with my grandfather and he would get me a hamburger and a Coke and then he'd sneak next door to (a bar named) The Spot for a beer." Did that bother Chris, that he'd been abandoned? "Oh, no," he says right out, "My grandfather was cool. He and I shared a lot of secrets."

But nothing lasts forever. By 1972 George and Mary were tired (George would pass away in 1976). They closed the Dixie. The facility was subsequently operated as a nightclub; then used for storage by nearby American Rentals. It was demolished circa 1992. On the site there is now a parking lot for a McDonald's.

Circa 1950 Postcard View

DUKE RESTAURANT — 112 and 114 East Sycamore — KOKOMO, IND.   7A-H3975

Circa 1950 Postcard View

Duke Restaurant
112-114 East Sycamore Street
Kokomo, Indiana

"Sugar cream was his trademark. If you wanted sugar cream pie you went to Jim Duke's. People would go down there, have a piece and smack their lips and say 'Let's have another piece.'" Such is Charles Sullivan's recollection of the Duke Restaurant. And Charles, now 76, should know: he's worked at the Victory Bicycle Shop, diagonally across from the site of Duke's, since 1939.

James "Jim" Duke was born in Taylor Township, just outside of Kokomo, in 1895. His dad died when Jim was 15, and Jim quit school to run the family farm for his mother and younger brothers and sisters. But restauranting was in Jim's blood. He left the farm in 1926 to start up a small eatery in Noblesville, just north of Indianapolis. From there it was a short hop, in 1929, up the road to Kokomo and a bigger restaurant in a bigger town.

At first Duke operated out of a rented space at 120 East Sycamore Street. But in 1932 he moved to his "dream" location, a large building at 112-114 East Sycamore that had been built in 1908 by the Kokomo, Marion & Western Traction (i.e., trolley) Company as their ticket office. It was ideal.

Reflects Kokomo historian and author Ned P. Booher: "In those days – before an avalanche of franchised food restaurants hit town – and with little competition, he (Jim Duke) built his operation into one of the best in the city." Continues Ned: "The Duke was famous for its sugar cream pie…which became known over a wide area. Even performers at the Sipe Theater, across the street, would dine at the Duke during every visit and, of course, wanted some of that pie." (Ed. note: for more on "that pie" please see pages 136-137.). Rita Rittenhouse, 65 and a former employee at the Duke, also well recalls the Duke's wonderful pies. But she remembers the restaurant's interior, too. "It was art deco and it was beautiful," she says with conviction.

At age 60, in 1955, Jim Duke closed his restaurant and retired. He died in August of 1968. His former location was home to Kokomo One Hour Martinizing, a dry cleaning firm, for most of the rest of the fifties. It was eventually torn down in the late 1970s. As Ned P. Booher puts it so well: "Another three story downtown building gone." The site is now a parking lot.

Dutch Mill Village
Route 31-E, South
Glasgow, Kentucky

The Great Depression of the 1930s served as the catalyst for many an ingenious idea. Such was certainly the case with Carroll "Ikey" Ream and his Dutch Mill Village.

A native of Paulding, Ohio, Ream had moved to Glasgow, about 90 miles directly south of Louisville, to play baseball for the semi-pro Glasgow Bruins in 1931. On the side he also managed a grocery store on Route 31-E, on the south edge of town.

When it became apparent that baseball would only take him so far, Ream began to concentrate on his grocery business. He purchased the property circa 1932 and began to note the tremendous number of cars that passed by each day, every day. He also noted that many of the cars were from out of state, tourists going to or from Florida or to or from nearby Mammouth Cave. Inspired by a friend, Frank Redford, who'd put together the highly successful Wigwam Village complex north of Glasgow, Carroll decided that he, too,

would create a one-stop-does-it-all combination of food, lodging, and gas (with souvenirs tossed in). Thus was born, in late 1936, Dutch Mill Village. As Carroll's son Jerry, 55, puts it, the idea was basic: "The windmills got your attention and got you to stop and eat. Then the next thing (while eating) would be, "Honey, let's spend the night here.""

It worked. With the gas pumps and the restaurant – which featured hand-cut steaks and what Carroll termed "Kentucky Kuisine" (which, Jerry smiles, translated to "country hams and home cooking") – in the big building nearest the highway and the cabins nestled behind, Carroll had a winner. As Jerry makes abundantly clear, however, his mother Eva had plenty to do with the Village's success. Explains Jerry: "The Dutch Mill was a 'Mom and Pop' business by definition. If Carroll was the visionary, then Eva made it go. Her labors were seemingly unending! Seven days a week she opened the

business at six a.m. for the breakfast crowd, later in the day she cooked pies and either helped or made the cabins, followed by working through the evening meal and many times closing up at eleven p.m. or midnight."

Carroll Ream died of a stroke in September 1962, but Eva kept the Dutch Mill going another 14 years, putting Jerry and his two brothers through college. The re-routing of Highway 31-E around Glasgow in the 1960s didn't help Eva or the business at all. In 1976 Eva treated her last customer, a regular named George White, to a free steak dinner, then locked the door behind him, and retired. Jerry says that day gave him a feeling of relief: "I'd seen how my parents slaved there." Eva died in May of 1990. The entire Village – every square foot of it - was eventually demolished. The site is now an open field. A man was selling produce under a tent the July day I was there.

DUTCH MILL VILLAGE   GLASGOW, KENTUCKY

Circa 1940 Postcard View

Circa 1940 Postcard View

Earl's Sandwich Shop
501 North Market St./Illinois Route 3
Waterloo, Illinois

Earl's is probably the "unfanciest" place included in this book. It was just a small, square cinder block building that sat "up at the Wedge," so-called because it's where three streets come together to form a triangle. It was a gas station first, then Earl's, then a gas station again, then gone. But its memory lingers on, and a beautiful July summer day spent talking with people in downtown Waterloo, located about 25 miles southeast of St. Louis in southern Illinois, was a most productive day.

"That was the place you could get a hamburger for cheap, really cheap" vividly recalls Jean Jost, 73 and a lifelong Waterloo resident. "It was kind of a hole in the wall. Real small." Clyde L. Burkhardt, 76 and also a local resident all his life, has much the same recollection: "It was a small place. You could hardly turn around. There were two or three small tables and a counter." But Clyde remembers, as well, the hamburgers ("They were good hamburgers.") and Earl ("Earl was very congenial."). It was Gloria Bundy, 75 and from nearby Maeystown, who had my favorite story. And she clearly loved telling it! Here's what Gloria had to say: "We used to go there (Earl's). We (Gloria and her husband-to-be, Guy) were dating. That was in the late thirties. We'd go to the movies at the Capitol Theater and then we'd go up to Earl's and buy six hamburgers for 25¢. They were little and they came in a small paper bag. And we'd each buy a bottle of soda for a nickel. We'd go to the show with a dollar. It was 25¢ each for the show, 25¢ for the six hamburgers, 10¢ for the two sodas...and we still had money for Sunday school."

Yep, Earl Gardner's hamburgers were cheap. But they were also good and tasty. "Real good...with sautéed onions on top" is how Gloria Bundy remembers them.

Local historian Bob Noelke, 82, recalls Earl's but he doesn't recall ever eating there. "I guess I didn't have the nickel," he chuckles. But some research on his part turned up a friend who remembered, as a kid in the mid-thirties, going to St. Louis with his grandfather. They passed up White Castle 5¢ hamburgers to come to Earl's "because they were better burgers. And they were served on bread rather than buns."

Earl's was in business for about a dozen years, from the early 1930s to 1944 or so. Bob Noelke thinks it closed because Earl, with wartime rationing, couldn't get enough meat. That makes sense: a hamburger stand without hamburger meat isn't likely to be a very happy stand. The building served as a filling station for a time after the War. It was demolished in the late 1940s. On the site there is now the Wedge Branch of the State Bank of Waterloo.

Fettrow's Grill
Junction of U.S. Routes 40 & 42
London, Ohio

Fettrow's Grill came into being because of the vision of one man, Paul D. Fettrow. A native of Pennsylvania, Fettrow first embarked on a journalistic career. And he was good at it, working his way up to State Editor of the *Harrisburg Telegraph* before deciding, in 1925, that running a restaurant was what he'd really rather be doing. Paul started in Amity Hall, a small town up the Susquehanna from Harrisburg. Giving evidence of what was to come, his place was a combination restaurant and filling station. As Donna Landis, Paul's granddaughter, tells it: "Mrs. Fettrow (Helen) cooked and Paul pumped gas by hand."

A motor trip in 1932 caused the Fettrows to leave Pennsylvania for Ohio: Paul fell in love with a stretch of land on the northern outskirts of London, 25 miles due west of Columbus. As Donna, somewhat dramatically, phrases it: "Probably millions of travelers had passed the intersection of U.S. Routes 40 and 42, but to them it was just a crossroads, a place to pass in a hurry. But to one traveler, Paul D. Fettrow, new opportunity was here and he began to dream a dream."

The dream became a reality on July 1, 1933: Fettrow's Grill opened its doors to the public. And the public responded. By stopping. And eating. And buying "That Good Gulf" gasoline. The business grew and, from their original one building and one acre, Paul and Helen eventually expanded to eight buildings and 44 acres. Included was a motel, a trucker's dorm, a Lubritorium, a garage, the restaurant, and not one but two filling stations. Paul and Helen changed the name of their endeavor from Fettrow's Grill to Fettrow Village.

It was the Grill, though, that was always the heart of the complex. Paul was especially proud of his ground beef sandwiches. He ground the beef himself every day. It was always fresh, never frozen. Helen was proud of her homemade pies and cinnamon rolls. They were both proud of their fresh vegetables (grown in a garden behind the restaurant) and their large portions. And that no one was ever turned away, even if he or she couldn't pay.

Eventually, though, hard times arrived at Fettrow's. Donna Landis again: "Thirty-five years passed. The new freeway (Interstate 70) was built and business became slow. Almost to a stop. Paul and Helen decided it was time to retire." In 1968 the couple moved to Holmes Beach, Florida, where Helen died in 1983; Paul in 1987. Their son William kept Fettrow's in operation until 1970, then sold it. The Grill building later served as a nightclub, and then a bar. Donna, who lives in London, says it was difficult for her to drive past it; "to see it deteriorate like it did."

Today only the motel, now called the R & R, yet stands. And it is in need of considerable attention. Everything else – including all that is shown in the postcard reproduced here – is gone.

FETTROW'S GRILL — NE. JUNCTION U. S. 40 AND 42 — NEAR LONDON, OHIO

Circa 1940 Postcard View

Circa 1950 Postcard View

Fort Raleigh Grill
601-603 East Main St./U.S. Route 17 (The Ocean Highway)
Elizabeth City, North Carolina

The tale of the Fort Raleigh Grill is a tale of two restaurants. Fort Raleigh number one opened its doors in 1936-37 at 107 North Poindexter Street in downtown Elizabeth City. Proprietors were John Kambis and Gus Geraris. It is this Fort Raleigh that 83-year-old Fred L. Fearing best recalls: "It was nothing fancy. Just an everyday, clean restaurant. No dancing girls. No strolling violinists. Just good food." Fred laughs as he recalls his favorite Fort Raleigh story: it seems that early in the restaurant's history a local semi-pro baseball team went to the Grill for dinner. There was this "humongous" watermelon on display in the restaurant's front window. One of the players picked it up and put it on his shoulder and told a teammate to go out for a pass. Player one then heaved it toward player two...who proceeded to miss it. There was watermelon chunks and seeds and juice everywhere. (Fred swears he was neither the tosser nor the tossee, but I have my suspicions!).

By 1948 the Fort had a new address and but one proprietor. The address was 601-603 East Main Street, in a corner building that had been home to an earlier eatery named the Puritan Grill. The sole proprietor was Gus Geraris. His specialties, based on ads of the day, were "Sea Foods and Sizzling Steaks." And you have to admire Gus' phone number. It was 1111. Not too awfully hard to remember. It is this Fort Raleigh, number two, that John Hale, 63, remembers: "I recall they had a big tank" and that in that big tank there were "exotic things like lobsters or other edible marine critters." John also remembers the restaurant as having "slow-turning fans."

Circa 1959 Angelo Mandos took over operation of the Fort Raleigh (by now called the Fort Raleigh *Restaurant* rather than the Fort Raleigh *Grill*). His reign lasted until 1963. In that year the Fort Raleigh was closed, and 601-603 East Main began a new life as Bradshaw's Jewelry Store.

All these years later the structure that served as Fort Raleigh number two is still occupied by Bradshaw's. It looks as it does in the postcard view pictured here. Sort of. It's still a two-story corner building. And the door and first floor windows are in the same location. But the attractive architectural ornamentation is gone. So, of course, is the signage. There is no lobster tank. And there are no rainbows.

Frank's Restaurant
Kessler Ave. & Summit St./Routes 77 & 90
Schulenburg, Texas

Deep in the heart of Texas is a place called Frank's. It could just as easily, though, be called Rozine's. Or, better yet, Frank & Rozine's.

It all began in 1929. That's the year Frank Tilicek, Sr., 23, and his wife Rozine, 19, opened the first Frank's. "It was just a little bitty cubbyhole," laughs Rozine, now 87, as she remembers back. Business was good, however, and in the early 1930s the couple moved into much more impressive surroundings...the Frank's pictured here. "I thought it was the prettiest building we've ever had," says Rozine. "I just liked the way it looked."

Most of the business – the restaurant was open 24 hours: Frank worked one 12-hour shift and Rozine the other – came from truck drivers. The initial menu featured 10¢ "Original Jumbo Hamburgers," soups, various chili dishes, pork chop dinner (35¢), ham steak dinner (50¢), and sandwiches (cheese, 10¢; ham & egg, 15¢; chicken salad, 15¢. Toasted bread cost 5¢ more.). The most expensive item was the chicken fried steak and it cost all of 60¢. It

was the hamburgers, though, that were the biggest success story. "Everybody else," recalls Rozine, "had 5¢ hamburgers, and Frank, Sr. had the idea of a jumbo 10¢ hamburger. They were so good. And large."

From the mid-thirties until World War II Frank's also featured carhops. That was Rozine's baby! "We had curb service and we were especially busy after the local dances. Cars would be all over." It's the uniforms, though, that gets Rozine to really beaming: "We had snappy uniforms. They were red and white satin. It was a real heavy satin. It looked like a majorette outfit. I was very particular about the right kind of uniform." Rozine was also very proud of the neon tubing that adorned the top of the restaurant. One night, more than any other, stands out. She was driving along Route 77 when the beauty of the lights overwhelmed her. "It was one of the highlights of my life," she says. "Seeing all those lights. It was something special for a small town in those days."

Frank, Sr. passed away unexpectedly in 1941, leaving Rozine to run things by her-

self until their son, Frank, Jr., stepped in to help in 1952. In 1959 Rozine and Frank, Jr. remodeled the building shown here. They enlarged, added a red brick exterior, added air conditioning. Within a decade, though, it was not enough. In the late 1960s Interstate 10 was constructed to replace Route 90 as the main thoroughfare between Houston and San Antonio. The Tiliceks knew they had a decision to make. "Our clientele is 90%-plus highway travelers," states Frank, Jr. "And we knew we had one of two choices: settle for a lot less business or (move and) go for broke." The family opted for the latter, opening their brand-new 10,000-square-foot restaurant just off the interstate in June 1970.

Today, with two more generations of Tiliceks pitching in, Frank's is a place of considerable renown in south-central Texas. Rozine is still on the scene as well: "I come in and eat my lunch (at the restaurant) every day," says she. "I enjoy coming and visiting with my friends." (Ed. note: for more on the Frank's of today – plus the Frank's pictured here – please see pages 116-117.).

Circa 1945 Postcard View

Circa 1950 Postcard View

Frisco Cafe
125 West 2nd St./Route 80
Odessa, Texas

It was difficult to miss the various statements that embellished the side wall of the Frisco Cafe's abode:

FAMOUS FOR FOOD

THIS IS IT!

GOOD FOOD

COURTEOUS SERVICE

CLEAN REST ROOMS

And the Frisco did, indeed, provide all of the above. For over two decades.

What was to become the Frisco Cafe was founded in 1940 as the Grill Cafe. Within a year, however, it had become the Frisco, with a man named C.H. Gauslin as proprietor. The "C" stood for Corrall.

Gauslin was a relative shorttimer: by 1945 Dee (for Dewitt) Crowell and John Held, Jr. were the Cafe's owners, and by 1947 Held was sole proprietor. It was under his direction that the Frisco Cafe enjoyed its grandest years. "The Frisco Cafe was one of the popular cafes in Odessa for many years." So says Jerri Fielding Sullivan, City Secretary, City of Odessa. Continues Jerri. "Many of the local roustabouts and roughnecks (Ed. note: roustabouts and roughnecks are people who work around oil wells. Odessa is BIG into oil.) would congregate there (at the Frisco) each morning waiting for the chance to go out on a rig. When one of them was hired, the Cafe would provide their lunch for that workday." Jerri also reports that many of Odessa's businessmen would gather at the Frisco every morning "for coffee and conversation."

In 1956 John Held, Jr. sold the Cafe to an Austrian native named Erica Markbreiter. Erica and the Frisco were old friends: she'd been the restaurant's manager since 1945. Completely on her own she ran it another seven years, until 1963. As with her predecessors, Erica kept the Cafe, still called the Frisco, open 24 hours a day, seven days a week. In fact, local legend has it that, when Erica finally closed the Cafe because of poor health, she had to call a locksmith to put a bolt on the door. It had never been locked!

The former restaurant was used for a time as the Door of Hope Mission, a non-denominational organization that provided food and lodging to people in need. It was eventually torn down. On the site there is now a one-story brick building that houses the law offices of Jimmy Edwards.

P.S. The words on the message side of the postcard pictured here – mailed by a person named L. Kline to the folks back home in Bristol, Tennessee, in May 1954 – read "Texas sure is a big state and plenty hot." It's an apt description.

George's
2588 South Highway 101/Pacific Coast Highway
Cardiff By The Sea, California

A long, long time before there was Interstate 5 hurtling motorists between San Diego and Los Angeles, there was Route 101, the Pacific Coast Highway. And there was George's.

George's was founded in 1916 by George Beech, a then 47-year old Englishman and longtime vaudevillian. How he came to be in Cardiff By The Sea and whether he fell head over heels in love with it is not known. It is known that he was able to purchase a choice piece of oceanfront property for rock bottom money. It was time to settle down.

At first George called his place George's Lobster Inn; later shortened to just plain George's. But he always liked to refer to it as "The House By The Side Of The Road" as well.

Growth was slow but steady until 1938 when Bing Crosby and a host of celebrity partners opened the Del Mar Thoroughbred Racetrack in nearby Del Mar. From then on growth was fast and steady. George's became THE spot for filmland's elite to dine as they made their way to or from the track. George's grandson, Bob San Clemente, can still rattle off a most impressive list of stars who dined at George's. It includes Bing, George Raft, Lana Turner, Jack Lemmon, Betty Grable, Pat O'Brien, Dorothy Lamour, Andy Devine, Mickey Rooney, Lucille Ball, Tony Curtis, Broderick Crawford, Alice Faye, Gregory Peck, and Mary Pickford and Douglas Fairbanks. Bob makes it clear the latter two were before his time. "My grandfather told me about them," he says. Another great memory of Bob's is his grandfather and Al Jolson gathered together for a duet around the restaurant's piano.

George Beech died in an automobile accident in 1939, and his son-in-law (and Bob's father), Mariano San Clemente, took over management. Bob started in five years later, while in high school. "I wanted to supplement my gasoline money," he laughs. By 1960 Bob could have all the gas money he wanted: he became the restaurant's owner and operator. One of his favorite recollections, in fact, is from that year. John F. Kennedy and several California colleagues stopped for dinner at George's on their way to San Diego to attend a Democratic rally. JFK commented it was the first time he'd eaten West Coast lobster. Smiles Bob: "He enjoyed it."

Bob decided to retire in 1975. "I was ready to get out of the restaurant/bar business," he says simply. He leased George's to Chart House, a decidedly upscale national chain. They promptly tore virtually all of the grand old restaurant down. One wall was kept standing so, as Bob explains, "It could be considered a remodel." (California law prohibits any new construction within 1,000 feet of the ocean.). Today's Chart House sits on the same location as did George's. Only it's bigger (6,000 square feet vs. 4,800) and, of course, it looks nothing at all like "The House By The Side Of The Road." (Ed. note: for more on the George's/Chart House of today please see page 111.).

100 miles from Los Angeles . . . CARDIFF BY THE SEA . . . 25 miles to San Diego

Circa 1940 Postcard View

Circa 1950 Postcard View

The Green Frog
102 Lee Ave./U.S. Route 1 Shortcut
Waycross, Georgia

Everyday places – such as restaurants and cafes – are seldom included in city or town histories. They are not, I guess, considered important enough. Such, though, is not the case with the Green Frog. In his spirited 1982 book on the history of Waycross, THIS MAGIC KINGDOM, author Robert L. Hurst pays very definite tribute to the Frog, its owners, its menu, its patrons. Much of the information that follows comes from that book.

The Green Frog came into being in 1938 when brothers Denham and William ("Bill") Darden, Sr. opened a small drive-in near the railroad underpass on the outskirts of downtown Waycross. Although geared primarily toward curb service, Denham and Bill, Sr.'s creation had an "inside," too. It consisted of a counter/soda fountain, two booths, and five stools, often jammed. Sundays were apt to be especially busy. As recalled by local columnist Jack Williams III years later in the Waycross *Journal-Herald:* "Many Waycrossans can remember being taken to the Frog's soda fountain by indulgent fathers and grandfathers for hot fudge sundaes." Five-cent Cokes and 15¢-sandwiches went over well, too.

During World War II the brothers added a twist to their curb service: they planted bamboo bushes in and around the parking lot. Patrons would drive in and wait for a carhop to appear out of the shrubbery. The seclusion was a delight to the many young couples who frequented the Frog. "Those bamboo stalks gained the reputation as 'giggle bushes,'" reflects Mr. Hurst, adding, "No explanation is needed." About the same time the Frog's motto – "Service With a Hop" – was born.

After the War the brothers expanded into a full-scale restaurant. The period from 1945 through the 1950s may well have been the Frog's golden years. Robert L. Hurst again: "The Green Frog became a place for coffee lovers in the morning, a lunchtime luncheon room for the noon hour crowd and an evening dinner occasion; it was the location for that first date, the memorable dinner before the senior prom, after-church get-together and just friends sharing a banana split. It was the Wednesday night fried chicken special and the Friday night fish fry. The Green Frog had earned its place as a landmark."

As the 1960s and 1970s arrived the Green Frog kept on growing. A special kids' section was added. So was the sale of alcoholic beverages. Eventually, though, the Dardens decided they were ready for new pastures. Orlando, Florida beckoned and the Dardens responded, moving operations there in late 1981. They served their last meal in Waycross in September. The September 22nd issue of the *Journal-Herald* featured an article by editor Jim Pinson that almost assuredly summed up the feelings of most people in the area: "Waycross and the Green Frog have been inseparable for lo these many years. It's been like two peas in a pod. Or like mustard and ketchup. Or like the Okefinokee and Swamp."

Today the Green Frog's former home sits near the railroad underpass on the outskirts of downtown Waycross. But that's where the resemblance begins and ends. The structure is now occupied by the Jones Company, and serves as headquarters for their Flash Foods chain of convenience stores. It has been completely remodeled and looks NOTHING like it did in its Green Frog days.

Griddle Cafe
401 West 5th St./Route 70
Plainview, Texas

The Griddle wasn't real fancy. It was a small stucco structure and possessed an oval counter and three booths on one side and two on the other. But it was a dream-come-true for Leroy "Bitsy" Newland. Newland had been a waiter (at the Busy Bee Cafe on East 6th Street). In 1939 he became a proprietor. His time as owner of the Griddle, however, was short. He joined the Coast Guard early on in World War II. Enter Faye Holder. She bought the Griddle from Newland. She enlarged it, too. Faye's daughter, Marie Kinnikin, 65, recalls that "Mother built a kitchen on the back, and she had carhops that worked out of back there. You could go inside or stay in your car." Barbeque was the specialty. Not surprisingly, the Griddle was largely a family business. "My brother cooked," continues Marie, and "I had two sisters, and we cooked and washed dishes and knew how to do everything." It was a non-family employee, Lilly Morgan, however, who probably made the greatest contribution to the success of the Griddle. Hired by Faye as a waitress and cook, it was Lilly who crafted the rolls and fruit cobblers for which the restaurant is still noted all these years later.

Faye Holder owned and operated the Griddle through 1954 when she retired, selling the business to a John Bley and his wife Loyce. Five years later, in 1959, the Bleys demolished the Griddle, replacing it with an entirely different building – on basically the same site – that they cleverly named the Nu-Griddle.

The Nu-Griddle carries on today, very much a tradition in and around Plainview (located in west Texas, approximately 80 miles south of Amarillo). It's owned by the husband and wife team of Paul Morgan and Mazie McCarty. That's certainly appropriate: Paul is Lilly Morgan's grandson. Even more appropriate is the fact that Lilly's rolls and homemade cobblers (cherry, apple, apricot, peach, purple plum, pineapple: take your pick!) are still as popular as they ever were. As Mazie reflects: "Times have changed, but not the Nu-Griddle. We still do it like grandma Morgan did it." (Ed. note: for more on the Nu-Griddle of today please see pages 118-119.).

Circa 1950 Postcard View

Hick's DRIVE-IN RESTAURANT
One mile south of Shively, on U. S. 31 W and 60 — LOUISVILLE, KY.

Circa 1950 Postcard View

Hick's Drive-In
4830 Dixie Highway/Routes 31W & 60
Louisville, Kentucky

Audrey Hicks, now 79, vividly recalls Derby Weekend (the first weekend in June; the weekend of the annual Kentucky Derby) of 1947. That was when her second son was born. And it was when her husband Edgar and his brother Dan opened their Hick's Drive-In. It was a good decision: postwar America was agog over the automobile. For the first time in history everybody seemed to own one; and everybody seemed to want to be in one as much as possible. Recalls Audrey: "The drive-in was new in that area (on the edge of Louisville in an area known as Pleasure Ridge Park) at that time. At night was when the young people enjoyed the carhop and getting to eat in their car. It drew people from miles and miles. The poor waitresses just ran all over themselves trying to take care of the people." Dorothy Schroerlucke vividly recalls those glory days as well. Now 68, Dorothy worked at Hick's as one of those "poor waitresses" in the late 1940s. "The restaurant was always full." she states. "There were times when it was just plain jammed."

The allure of Hick's, though, was not just the novelty of it. For one thing, it was beautiful. Audrey Hicks again: "The building was circular, and the interior was all glass. The counter was horseshoe-shaped, and under the counter there were clear glass squares and there were colored neon lights behind it. On the outside there was beautiful shrubbery." Adds Dorothy Schroerlucke: "There was a tremendous amount of chrome in the restaurant. I," she laughs, "recall it well because we had to keep it shined up." Sums up Audrey: "That was the talk for a long time…about how beautiful the restaurant was."

People talked about the food, too. Audrey recollects that Hick's served "a beautiful breakfast." But she just about drools as she remembers the dinners, too. Especially the steaks. "They were really famous for their steaks," she smiles. Another satisfied eater was Frances Troutman, now 64. "I used to go there with my sweetie, Andrew. He later became my husband. We usually double-dated with another couple, Birdie and Eddie. We would go there (Hick's) coming home from going to a movie. To go there was really a treat." And here Frances gets quite excited: "They had the greatest cheeseburgers in the world. They were humongous. It was served in a little plastic basket. And the French fries were twice as many as you get now and they were so good!"

In time bad blood came between Edgar and Dan. Edgar bowed out, leaving Dan to run Hick's alone. It was too much. In 1958 Dan sold Hick's to a regional chain called Jerry's. Today, greatly, remodeled – and not looking the least like the view shown here – it is still operated as a Jerry's. (Ed. note: for more on the building of today please see page 110.).

Hollywood Grill
500 Main Street
Dubuque, Iowa

Hollywood came to Dubuque – by way of Greece – in 1941. That's the year brothers Gus and Spiro Bogas, along with partner Dan Diamond, opened the Hollywood Grill in the thick of things in downtown Dubuque. All three were natives of Greece; all three were old hands in the restaurant business. The Hollywood was to be their masterpiece. By all accounts it was.

The Hollywood, as remembered by family member and former employee George Bogas, was best noted for its soda fountain, complete with homemade ice cream and homemade toppings. You could also, though, treat yourself to just about any short order meal your heart might desire…especially if your desire were ham. George clearly pictures an ever-present Dubuque ham: "You could always see that ham standing in a rack on the chef's work counter if you peeked in through the front window." George also recalls the partners' motto: "If you come in here and are the only customer, then dinner for you is on the house."

It would appear not many dinners were given away. I spoke with a host of people in "The Heidelberg of America." They all remembered the Hollywood Grill. Bill Lynn, 68, recalled that the meal was always good, the jukebox had a fine selection, and the booths had "big seat cushions." For Don Dahms, 62, it was also the well-padded booths. "There were real comfortable," he fairly sighed. "It was one of the nicest places in that part of town," Elmer Schiel, 72, told me. Jeannine Kersch, 61, best recalls co-proprietor Dan Diamond: "He had a big, bushy head of hair and he was very outgoing, very talkative." My favorite interview, though, was with 74-year-old Muriel Schemmel, whom I approached while she was out for a stroll with her dog. Muriel's eyes lighted up when I asked her about the Hollywood. And it was the ham that did it: "In the front window they always had a baked ham studded with cloves and glazed with brown sugar, cherries, and pineapple rings. It was on a big platter. And they'd have flowers surrounding it. It was gorgeous." Did Muriel ever have any of the ham? You bet: "We used to sit in the booths after shopping. We'd stop in for a ham sandwich. It was always very good."

Dan Diamond and the Bogas brothers operated the Hollywood until 1956 when it was purchased by the mother and son team of Bernadette and Raymond Engling. Actually, though, nobody called her Bernadette. It was always "Ma," in recognition of the fact she had 14 children (seven boys and seven girls!). Gus Bogas re-bought the Grill in 1963, changing its name to the Town House Restaurant. In 1970 the building was converted into offices for the American States Insurance Company. In 1971 it was torn down as part of an Urban Renewal project. On the site there is now a parking lot.

**Circa 1950
Postcard View**

17185

HOPKINS DINOR
219 Pennsylvania Avenue, W.
Warren, Pa.

Circa 1940 Postcard View

Hopkins Dinor
219 Pennsylvania Avenue, West
Warren, Pennsylvania

No, you're not seeing things. It really does say Hopkins Dinor. For as long as anyone can recall many diners in northwestern Pennsylvania, western New York, and even parts of eastern Ohio and West Virginia's northern panhandle have had their name spelled with an "o" rather than an "e." There are several reasons espoused as to why. Most are variations on the theme "Somebody spelled it that way years ago and we've just been doing it the same ever since." The answer is that nobody really knows for sure.

Actually, not knowing for sure is the perfect introduction to Hopkins: it can safely be said that it, too, is an entity that nobody really knows for sure about. It was certainly the most frustrating research topic in this book. City directories (similar to telephone books, but with more information), local histories, the daily newspaper, and old copies of THE DRAGON, Warren High's yearbook, all make no mention of the Hopkins or contain any ads for it. A full day and a half of talking with people "of age" – on the street, in bars and restaurants, in the library, and in the senior citizens' center – yielded no recollections, either.

Here's what *is* known. In 1925 a diner/dinor arrived at 219 Pennsylvania Avenue, West. It was called the American Dining Car, with Emily and Richard Joseph as proprietors. It operated for but a year or so. The name was then changed to Riche's Dining Car, with Elmer Richardson the proprietor. There were no further changes until 1933, when Aletta Richardson, Elmer's wife (probably Elmer's widow), took over as proprietor. Aletta and Riche's continued along until 1940. Then nothing. No Riche's, no Aletta, no listing for any structure at 219 Pennsylvania Avenue, West.

My strong hunch: that someone named Hopkins bought the dining car in late 1940 or early 1941 and ran it just about long enough to have it "pose" for the wonderful postcard view shown here. They then vanished, perhaps taking the diner/dinor with them. This hunch is somewhat substantiated by older people around Warren who recall Riche's ("They had fabulous food," Lucy Notoro, age 75; "It reminded me of a streetcar," Charles Greenlund, age 82; "It wasn't anything exotic: it was good for a light lunch," Harry Speidel, age 74) and recall it as looking very similar to the view of Hopkins. It is *not* substantiated by any "Hopkin" or "Hopkins" listed in the Warren city directory. Then again, a directory wasn't published every year. (There was none for 1941, as an apt example.).

About the only thing known for sure is that there is nothing resembling the Hopkins Dinor now occupying 219 Pennsylvania Avenue, West. What is there is a newish-looking building that is home to Jarvis Cleaners (One is tempted to make that "Cleanors."), a dry cleaning establishment.

Kentland Cafe
North 4th & East Graham Sts./Routes 24, 41, & 52
Kentland, Indiana

The Kentland Cafe was located in Kentland, Indiana, a not-very-sizable community in the northwestern corner of Hoosierland. It could, however, just as easily have been located in Kentland, Idaho. Or Kentland, New Hampshire. Or Kentland, Mississippi. For the Kentland Cafe was Kentland, America in terms of its being an archetypal high school gathering place of the 1930s through the 1960s. Archie, Betty, Veronica, Jughead; Henry Aldrich; Corliss Archer; Judy Foster and Oogie Pringle; Ricky Nelson; even Richie Cunningham and the Fonz: all would have loved the Kentland Cafe.

Local historian Janet Miller loves the Kentland Cafe, too. "In its heyday," she reports, "the Cafe was commonly referred to as the 'K.C.' It was a hangout for kids and adults alike after a Kentland (High School) Blue Devils' ballgame of any sort. When the team would come in everyone would clap and cheer whether the team won or lost."

It's everybody's old favorite pranks, however, that Janet clearly enjoys the most. Me, too. "The boys used to love to play jokes on the waitresses at the K.C. One favorite was to mix the salt and pepper together. Also the salt and sugar." (The latter, Janet laughs, caused at least one patron to start drinking her coffee black.) "Another trick was to turn a glass of water upside-down on a piece of waxed paper and then slide it back on the table and pull out the waxed paper. This," notes Janet, "left the waitress in a quandary as to how to pick up the glass without spilling the water all over the table." Ah, such fun.

What made the K.C. so attractive to the area's youths was its coziness (mostly its booths), its jukebox, and, of course, its food. You could get a T-bone steak, fried chicken, or fried catfish. More apropos, you could get hamburgers, French fries, peanut butter and jelly sandwiches, and milkshakes.

While best remembered for its hoards of teenagers, the Kentland, which opened in 1931, served many an adult, too. This was especially true every Memorial Day. Explains Janet: "The restaurant was located on U.S. Highway 41. It was a direct route from Indianapolis to Chicago. After the Indianapolis 500 this road was bumper to bumper with cars heading north. In days of old the race ended at about 4:00 PM and the crowds began to reach Kentland about 7:00 PM. The K.C. stayed open 24 hours at this time to accommodate the crowd. Many town and country people in the area parked along the streets to watch the traffic coming through town."

Well, there isn't much traffic to watch coming through town any more. Interstate 65 saw to that. The K.C. shut its doors circa 1960. The building that housed it, however, still stands. It's been used as an oil company office, an insurance company office, and an antique shop. It's today occupied by a pizza parlor. (Ed. note: for more on the K.C.'s building of today please see page 112.).

KENTLAND CAFE — KENTLAND, INDIANA

Circa 1950 Postcard View

Madison Diner

Route 38, Mt. Holly, N. J.

Circa 1950 Postcard View

Madison Diner
1570 Route 38
Mount Holly, New Jersey

The Madison's slogan was "Meet Your Friend at the Madison Diner." And for a time it seems as if everybody did meet there. Ron Tubertini, son of longtime proprietors Herman and Mary Tubertini, recalls when both the diner and its parking lot were full up. "Route 38 was home to many car dealers," states Ron, "so the diner was *the* lunch spot for a number of car salesmen and mechanics. Also area farmers. The lot was also filled with PSE&G (Public Service Electric & Gas) trucks as well as New Jersey Bell and various other truckers who would fill both the parking lot and diner at any time."

The Madison was originally located in Burlington, New Jersey, just before the entrance to the Burlington-Bristol Bridge. It was purchased and moved circa 1945 by James Becker, who owned both a Chrysler-Plymouth dealership and a bowling alley on Route 38, just across the highway from the diner's new location in Mount Holly (located in south central New Jersey, about 25 miles east of Philadelphia). Becker bought the diner to set up good friends Floss and Ed Bowker in the food business. But Floss and Ed ran into financial difficulties almost from the start. To help, Becker built a dining room addition (shown to the right in the postcard view), and his wife Helen moved in and managed operations until they were back on a fairly even keel. Nevertheless, by 1950 the Beckers decided it was time to get out of the diner business. They sold the Madison to the Tubertinis.

Ron remembers that all the food at the diner was prepared by Herman, starting at 3:00 AM every day. Almost everything was homemade. Herman was especially known for his navy bean soup. But "Whatever he cooked up was good," exclaims Joe Gerdelman, 63. Joe ought to know: he worked right across the road from the diner and enjoyed many a meal there back in the 1950s. "You'd go there in the morning and he always had quite a crowd," says Joe. "Lunchtime, too. He was," sums up Joe with not the least trace of hesitation, "the greatest cook in the world."

In the early 1960s Herman and Mary replaced the diner pictured here with a new (and, let it be noted, far less attractive) model. This they operated until finally calling it quits and retiring in the late 1970s.

The structure that was Madison Diner #2 still exists at its same old stand on Route 38. Now, however, it's a Chinese place, the Cozy Restaurant. Navy bean soup is not on the menu. (Ed. note: for more on today's structure please see page 109.).

Marilorn Barbeque Route 17, East Waverly, New York

"Are you going to renovate it?" asked Janet Keene, Deputy Clerk for the Town of Barton, when I showed up to inquire about the Marilorn. "If you are," she continued somewhat breathlessly, "I'd be the first one to give you business." Janet then raved about the Marilorn's barbeque; how she and her husband-to-be Ron would drive up in his 1949 pink and white Chevy; how they enjoyed the carhop service. She was disappointed when I told her "No," that I wasn't planning on renovating the Marilorn.

Located on the Waverly-Barton town line approximately 40 miles west of Binghamton and just north of Athens, Pennsylvania, the Marilorn Barbeque goes back to the 1930s. Original owners were Mary and Lauren (as in Marilorn) Pierce. Then, in 1945, came Mabel Michaels. Mabel advertised home cooking, Texaco gas, and cabins with Simmons beds, running water (hot and cold), showers, and private toilets. Added to the cabin particulars was the statement "We cater to tourists only."

Mabel sold the Marilorn to husband and wife Helen and Tony Daddona in 1950. "We were known for our Texas hots, our barbeque, and our carhop and curb service," reminisces Helen. Of the three it's easy to tell which she was proudest of. "We switched barbeque recipes when we took over," she says right off. "We felt our recipe was much better." Patrons seemed to agree. "People are still talking about it," states Helen. "It was different."

Under the Daddonas the Marilorn was open from early May until Labor Day. When asked if it was fun, Helen replies that "It was hard work but we had a lot of young people as customers and they really enjoyed coming." They'd bring their dates, she recollects back. "Even the older people enjoyed it. We were on the outskirts of town and it was really nice."

Helen and Tony ran the Marilorn until 1967 when they decided it was time to retire. They leased the place for awhile. But that didn't work out and the couple just closed things down.

Today, while the cabins are gone (Helen: "We sold the cabins individually. People bought them and carted them off to use as storage space and the like."), the other buildings pictured here still stand. The former tourist home (the large building to the right) is rented out as apartments, while the former restaurant is utilized for storage. (Ed. note: for more on the buildings of today please see page 113.).

SINGLE AND DOUBLE CABINS

THE MARILORN BARBECUE AND TOURIST HOME — ROUTE No. 17 — WAVERLY, N. Y.

Circa 1945 Postcard View

Circa 1945 Postcard View

Oklahoma Joe's
1720 East Central Ave./Route 66
Albuquerque, New Mexico

Oklahoma Joe's had what could almost be called a split personality. Persona number one was geared to tourists. And food. Persona number two was geared to students. And beer.

Let's start with number one and Alma Patton. She's the person who began Oklahoma Joe's in 1935. She didn't call it Oklahoma Joe's, though. She called it the Dixie Barbeque. She didn't stay with it very long, either. Within two years she'd sold the Dixie to a man named Joe Feinsilver. Route 66 was being re-routed to come down Central Avenue and Joe knew a good thing when he saw it. Joe's next move, in 1941, was to change the name of his place to Oklahoma Joe's. He kept the name "Dixie Barbeque," too. In fact, according to the wording on the address side of the postcard pictured here, the restaurant's full name was Oklahoma Joe's Dixie Genuine Pit Barbeque

("All food supervised by Oklahoma Joe in person.").

Somewhere along the way, most likely in the years following World War II, Oklahoma Joe's became Okie Joe's, a hangout for University of New Mexico students. A beer joint. Mo Palmer of the Albuquerque Museum reasons that this phenomenon occurred as the city's streets were widened to accommodate the ever-increasing traffic flow. Mo's theory is that wider streets meant smaller parking lots and smaller parking lots meant that tourists just kept on driving.

This, persona number two if you will, is what most older Albuquerque folks recall when asked about memories of Oklahoma Joe's. It's always "Okie Joe's" (or just plain "Okie's") and it's always beer. Local history buff Marie Hays, 80, probably describes Okie Joe's as well as anyone: "When the sun set Okie's came alive. 'Meet you at

Okie's' was the thing to say and do. Beer was cheap, the jukebox loud, and there were always lots of Lobos (Ed. note: "Lobos" is the nickname for University of New Mexico students.) to party with. Sandwiches and snacks were sold, but beer and fun were the main attractions. It was," sums up Marie, "the typical college hangout of the postwar period."

In 1956 Joe Feinsilver bowed out of his longtime establishment, selling to a George Robbins. Robbins immediately changed the name to Oklahoma Joe's Bar & Restaurant. A year later he changed it again, to the Robbins Inn. It was back to Okie Joe's in 1959, and a variation on that theme through 1981. The structure was demolished in 1982 to make way for Seven-Eleven Convenience Store #23,220. Today the Seven-Eleven, augmented by a Fina gas station, still adorns the site where tourists — and later Lobos — met.

One Spot Cafe
768 North Broadway Blvd./Routes 40 & 81
Salina, Kansas

It's seen five names and almost sixty years but the structure pictured here is still going strong. Originally named Sprout's Cafe by initial proprietor John W. Sprout, it was constructed in 1939. Lifelong Salina resident Harley Herrington yet well recalls that construction: then all of 12 years old, he helped with the laying of the concrete floor. Harley, who's still a regular at the restaurant today, recalls that it was 110° and the concrete was drying as fast as the crew was pouring it.

Circa 1945 John W. Sprout got out of the restaurant business and Sprout's Cafe became the One Spot Cafe, so-called, according to local lore, because it was the only eating place located thereabouts. If you wanted a square meal it was the one spot on that stretch of old Highway U.S. 40 where you could find one!

The One Spot it was and the One Spot it remained – under numerous proprietors and managers – until 1968 when new owners Lola and Spencer Stewart concluded that the name Big Key Cafe was to be their ticket to success. Lola and Spencer also converted a rear pantry into an additional dining room.

Two name changes later – to Trails Restaurant in 1985, and to Trails End Restaurant in 1991 – brings us to the present. And to today's proprietor, Debbie Werber. Debbie, who took over both ownership and operation in August 1996, describes her place as "the working man's restaurant." Large portions are the order of the day. "If you leave hungry it's your own fault," she laughs. Debbie's proud, too, that a goodly number of the restaurant's original customers – customers who go back to the One Spot and even Sprout's – still come in every day. "And," she adds, "if they don't come in for a day or two we go looking for them" (to make sure they're ok.).

"As long as this restaurant has been in operation," states Debbie in conclusion, "homemade cinnamon rolls, homemade pies, and real home cooking have been the name of the game. The present owner does not plan to change any of these trademarks." (Ed. note: for more on the Trails End of today please see pages 120-121.).

One Spot Cafe

HI-WAYS 81 & 40

SALINA, KANSAS

Coca-Cola

SANDWICHES   MEALS   SHORT ORDERS   Coca-Cola

ONE SPOT CAFE
FAIRMONT
ICE CREAM

ONE SPOT CAFE

FRIED CHICKEN

PARTY ROOM

P·I·E   I·E   P·I·E

Circa 1955 Postcard View

Circa 1945 Postcard View

Penn State Flyer
801-809 Union Blvd./Route 22
Allentown, Pennsylvania

There was once an automobile – the 1947-1949 Studebaker – that was sometimes called "the backwards-forwards car." That's because it could be difficult to tell whether it was coming or going. Well, the Penn State Flyer was a Sterling Streamliner (manufactured by the J.B. Judkins Co., of Merrimac, Massachusetts) and it could be called "the backwards-forwards diner." There certainly was a strong resemblance between the Streamliner and a sleek locomotive. But was it coming or going?

As sleek as it was, though, the Penn State Flyer is not much recalled in "The Queen City of the Lehigh Valley" today. I approached at least 20 people who were obvious oldsters. Only two had any recall. One of the two, however, was four-term (16 years!) former mayor Joseph Daddona. That seemed special. His Honor, now 64, recollected the Penn State as a "landmark" and a beautiful one. "It impressed me," he stated, "because it looked like our trolley cars." Joe was also impressed with the food. He worked nearby and often ate there. "You could get a full meal or something quicker. It was all excellent."

The other recollection belonged to Kathy Guth, age 73. Kathy used to rollerskate by the diner as a teenager in the early 1940s. ("After school, of course," she laughs. "I never skipped school, I was a very good person."). She recalls that the Flyer looked just as it does in the postcard view except that it didn't have all the flowers and shrubbery shown in the view. (Ed. note: postcard artists *were* known to add things like blue sky and shrubs and subtract things like clouds and fire hydrants.). "It seemed to be doing a good business," she told me.

The Penn State Flyer's stay in Allentown was not as long as it might have been. And definitely not as long as it should have been. Some people, according to diner historian Larry Cultrera, believe that the Flyer had a previous life in State College, a community located in central Pennsylvania and the home of Penn State University. That would make sense, given the diner's "Penn State" appellation. And diners certainly are quite transportable. It *is* known that the diner arrived in Allentown in 1941. Proprietor number one was Anthony Mangino, a 56-year-old native of Naples, Italy. Four proprietors later the Flyer's time in Allentown had run out. It was purchased in May of 1956 by diner veterans James Durkin and Clarence Smith, both residents of Scranton. The purchase price was $30,000. A year later the partners moved their treasure to Scranton where it was operated as Yank's Diner for a time.

There is today no Yank's Diner in Scranton. Does, however, the old Flyer still exist in one form or another in or around Scranton/Wilkes-Barre? Or State College? Or Allentown?

I'd like to think that it does. (Ed. note: the first diner to have been placed on the National Register of Historic Places is the Modern Diner, located in Pawtucket, Rhode Island. It is a Sterling Streamliner.).

Pete's Cafe
314 Main Street/Route 40
Boonville, Missouri

When asked why he came to America, Greek native Pete Christos would reply it was because he'd "heard the streets were paved with gold." When asked why he came to Boonville, he would reply "because it's where the good Lord wanted me."

Pete came to America – and Boonville, located in central Missouri, about 100 miles directly east of Kansas City – when he was 15 years old. In 1911. By day he shined shoes. By night he slept in the barber chair in the barbershop in which he worked. His dream: to save enough money to open his own eating place.

It was a dream that came true in 1920 when Pete bought an existing confectionery shop at 321 Main Street in the heart of Boonville and transformed it into Pete's Candy Kitchen. Pete's son, Pete II, recalls the Candy Kitchen of those early years as "modest; serving ice cream, fountain drinks, and sandwiches." (Plus candy, of course.). By the latter part of the decade Pete's horizons were widened: a 1927 ad promised "A Great

Big Dinner for 35¢," and especially touts the restaurant's special 50¢ Sunday dinner. ("If you have never tried it you have a pleasant surprise awaiting you.").

In 1935 Pete's horizons widened even more. He moved operations to more spacious surroundings in a former saloon at 314 Main Street. Pete's Candy Kitchen had become Pete's Cafe.

The Cafe was a Main Street delight. With its huge neon sign and its cream and black Carrara glass (similar to milk glass, only colored) exterior it brightened the entire block. Pete brightened Route 40, too. In fact, some might say he was about as famous for the red diamond–shaped signs he erected along U.S. 40 from Indianapolis to Hays, Kansas as he was for his food. "People would follow those signs all the way to Boonville," Pat Jackson of the Chamber of Commerce will tell you.

Pete, says his son with obvious pride, was an innovator. He had the first air conditioning in town. Also the first neon lighting.

More important, says Pete II, is that Pete's Cafe was the first eating place in Missouri to serve people of all races and colors.

The years went by. The year 1960 arrived. It was not a good year for Pete's Cafe. Pete Christos died in November, age 64. And the decision had been made to move to a location adjacent to newly-constructed Interstate 70. It was a bad move. Pat Jackson again: "People were afraid when the interstate came through. Two miles (to downtown) seemed like such a long distance. If Pete had only realized that people would come. Business was never the same after they moved out of downtown."

The new Pete's – the one out by the interstate – closed in 1970. The Pete's pictured here – THE Pete's – was combined with 316 Main and converted to a Dollar Store. Then a Sears. Then a bar. It is now, long stripped of its Carrara glass and its beauty (and the ice cream machine in the window, too), boarded up and for sale. Call Susie Thoma at (816) 882-5908 if you'd like to take a look.

PETE'S AIR-CONDITIONED CAFE

PETE'S
CAFE
SODAS
BEER
AIR
CONDITIONED
CAFE

SODAS PETE'S CAFE

314

Pete's Cafe
AIRCONDITIONED

9A-H684

**Circa 1940
Postcard View**

314 MAIN STREET   BOONVILLE, MISSOURI

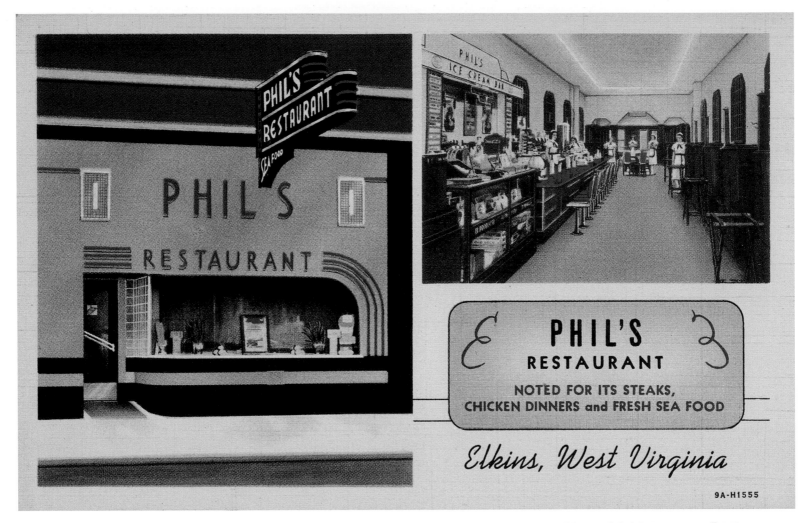

PHIL'S RESTAURANT
SEA FOOD

PHIL'S
RESTAURANT

PHIL'S
ICE CREAM BAR

PHIL'S
RESTAURANT
NOTED FOR ITS STEAKS,
CHICKEN DINNERS and FRESH SEA FOOD

Elkins, West Virginia

9A-H1555

Circa 1940 Postcard View

Phil's Restaurant
305-307 Davis Ave./Routes 33, 219 & 250
Elkins, West Virginia

He laughs now. But you may be certain he didn't find it side-splitting then. "He" is Willard "Phil" Phillips and "it" was his adventures with his waitress staff. "When you had that many girls working for you," laments Phil, "you had a little of everything. We even had some hairpulling and some dish throwing at times. You heard about all their boyfriends, where they were the night before, and where they were going that night." It was, of course, the first job for many of Phil's charges, made especially difficult by the fact that "they were often being approached by young male customers." Phil tried to solve that one by hiring married women…only to discover one year that he had five waitresses who were working solely to make money to get a divorce.

Phil's Restaurant was the handiwork of the "original" Phil, Phil Goldman. Goldman, who'd earlier been proprietor of a clothing store in Elkins (located in the eastern part of the state, approximately 150 miles west of Washington, D.C.), opened his eatery in 1929. For the first year of its being it was your basic soda fountain/sandwich shop. In 1930, however, Elkins staged a huge Forest Festival and Phil found himself serving complete meals to the visiting multitudes. He liked the feeling. The result: Phil began to focus increasingly on full-meal trade; even expanded his floor space.

In 1943 Phil #2, Willard "Phil," entered the scene. He bought the restaurant. "I never changed the name," he says, "because my name was Phillips and everyone called me Phil." In addition, notes Phil #2, "The name 'Phil's' had a good reputation and all the china had the name ('Phil's') on it. Plus all the advertising and promotional material had 'Phil's' on it, too. It would have been impossible to replace during the war."

In 1946 Phil (Phillips) went whole hog: he did away with the soda fountain, completely remodeling into a full-scale operation. "I wanted a full-menu customer instead of just a Coke or a coffee or a slice of pie customer," he puts it. The new Phil's was a smash success. Of course, it almost had to be. Phil Phillips had, after all, been in the restaurant business since his high school graduation in 1932. After scoring success in his hometown of Junior, West Virginia, he made the move to Elkins in 1938 to manage the Moose Club; then the Elks Club; then Phil's.

Phil – with help from his brother Eustace – operated Phil's right through to 1967. Since then the space has been used as a cafeteria, an antique shop, and, per Phil, "other short-lived endeavors." In early 1997 it was remodeled into part of an upscale eating and drinking establishment known as C.J. Maggies.

All these years later what does Phil Phillips – who still resides in Elkins – recall most about his restaurant? His answer is three-fold: the employees ("They were like family."), the up-to-dateness (Phil's was the first business in Elkins to be air-conditioned, and the first to use fluorescent lighting, too.), and his Broiled Filet of Sirloin Steak. "It was," he says simply, "the very best." (Ed. note: for more on the building of today please see page 113.).

Pilot Cafe
1726 West North Temple St./Route 40
Salt Lake City, Utah

"They used to have cowboys who would – as a joke – ride in right through the front door. Hootin' and hollerin'. The owner would laugh and chase them out. Outside was a flagpole and the cowboys would tie their horses and come back in." So recalls Shirley Newman, laughing all the way. And Shirley's seen a lot of the Pilot Cafe, both as an employee and customer, in her 56 years.

The Pilot was launched by E.L. "Ed" Allen, Sr., who'd previously owned and operated restaurants in Pocatello, Idaho and elsewhere in Salt Lake. When it was built the Pilot was, in the words of local historical researcher David C. Buhler, "out in the boondocks." Downtown Salt Lake was far away. The Cafe, as a result, was not a place that was frequented by many. Its greatest draw was its proximity to the airport. People, again per David, would go out and "watch the planes come in and take off" and then stop at the Pilot for a meal afterwards.

Patrons had a choice of being served inside or being waited on by carhops outside.

In its early years Pilot's may have been better known as a dance hall. Indeed, interior photos taken in May of 1943 show a large hardwood dance floor surrounded by padded booths. Also clearly in evidence is a bandstand and a jukebox. Other interior shots from the same date show an inviting dining room, complete with western-scene murals and checkered tablecloths, and a spacious counter area with supposed-to-be-smiling (but they weren't!) waitresses, and signs that advertised "Choice Tender Steaks," "Bar-B-Q Pig Ribs (In The Rough/Served Without Silver)," "Hot Turkey Sandwich," "Sundaes And Malts," and "Chicken In The Rough." The latter was the house specialty. An early 1944 ad, in fact, ballyhoos the Pilot's Chicken in the Rough as "That fried chicken plate that took the states by storm." The ad goes on to describe the dish as "One-half unjointed fried chick-

en, gobs of shoestring potatoes, hot buttered roll, and honey." All served without silverware. (Ed. note: Chicken in the Rough was a copyrighted name, the brainstorm of a man named Beverly Osborne and first served in his restaurant in Oklahoma City in 1936.).

By the 1950s Salt Lake had grown to the point where the Pilot had more of a neighborhood surrounding it. The cafe became more of a neighborhood cafe. Cowboys notwithstanding, that's the way Shirley Newman remembers it. Shirley, who's worked at the Pilot or its successors for 30 years, also remembers the restaurant's "really good hamburgers...big gigantic hamburgers."

In the years since the 1950s all or part of the Pilot's structure has been utilized as a private club, a bowling alley, a Japanese restaurant. It is today – greatly remodeled – a private dance club called Club Shakers. (Ed. note: for more on the building of today please see page 109.).

Circa 1950 Postcard View

PURITY CAFE

On U. S. Highways 77 and 166

Circa 1945 Postcard View

Purity Cafe
124 South Summit St./Routes 77 & 166
Arkansas City, Kansas

You don't have to speak many words of English to create a good meal, a fact not wasted on a multitude of Greek immigrants. The result: from Albuquerque to Dubuque to Elizabeth City to Boonville there's a lot of Greek success stories in this book. Add Arkansas City to the list.

The three Gochis Brothers – Louis, Pete, and Gus – arrived in the U.S.A. from their native Greece as teenagers circa 1910. At first they were scattered, but in 1918 Pete discovered Arkansas City (located in southern Kansas approximately 50 miles southeast of Wichita; pronounced R-can-sas City; often called Ark City). He thought it held great promise for a family business. He was right.

That same year, 1918, the brothers purchased the already-in-existence Purity Candy Kitchen at 309 South Summit Street in downtown Ark City. The business prospered and in 1939-1940 Pete and Louis (Gus had dropped out of the picture) moved their endeavor to larger space at 124 South Summit and renamed it the Purity Cafe. Their formula for success, though, remained the same. Pete and his wife Goldie handled the menu, the cooking, and the kitchen staff. Louis and his wife Velda took care of the finances. One of the brothers was on the premises at all times.

Eighty-year-old lifelong Arkansas City resident Fitzgerald F. Harder well recalls 124 South Summit: "The new location was well situated. All four of the town's movie theaters were less than a block away. After the show, or before it, it was customary to have one's date enjoy a meal or a sandwich at the Purity." The Purity was also a business rendezvous. "The new Purity became the town's focal point," continues Fitzgerald Harder. "When appointments were made it was often 'Meet you at the Purity.' "

Patricia Gochis Stigers, Pete and Goldie's daughter, has memories, too. "The restaurant featured handcut steaks, prime rib, fresh seafood, homemade soup, pies, doughnuts, hot breads, and wonderful homemade ice cream. There were specials every day. Greek dishes would be prepared upon special request."

Waitresses wore the traditional garb of the day: a light pink apron over a white dress, with the apron tied in the back in a large bow. And, notes Fitzgerald Harder, "They were never ever without their menu booklet."

Pete Gochis died in 1963, and in 1968 the Purity suffered a fire that destroyed most of its interior. Louis and new partners Nick and Bill Argos decided it would be too costly to rebuild. Louis retired. He died in 1985.

The Purity's 124 South Summit structure was demolished in the 1970s. On the site there is now a one-story addition to adjacent Home National Bank. The Purity's first location, a two-story building at 309 South Summit, still stands. The top floor is boarded up. The ground floor is occupied by Mylissa's Garden Antiques.

Royal Cafe and Drive-In
205 Avenue F/Route 90
Del Rio, Texas

The little gem of a cafe pictured here was the creation of a man whose name was Adolphus J. Gallemore, but whom everybody simply called "A.J." He was a character, best remembered as a very large man who would ride around town in a jumpsuit or coveralls on a horse or in his big Cadillac car. He loved to shout and was known to walk into the bank and yell out whatever was on his mind. One time a bank examiner – described as "a meek, mild bank examiner" – was up on the mezzanine doing what bank examiners do and in strolled A.J., who let out with a roar. "It," as people around town still remember, "just about scared the poor man half to death." Legend has it, too, that one Sunday A.J. walked up the aisle of the Baptist church and sat right behind the pulpit while the preacher gave his sermon.

A.J. came to Del Rio (located on the Mexican border in southwestern Texas, 155 miles straight west of San Antonio) during World War II to work as a pharmacist at a local drug store. By War's end, however, he was out of pharmaceuticals and into fried chicken and K.C. steaks. "They served regular west Texas food: steaks, hamburgers, fried chicken," recalls Betty Tidwell, 74, who ran a nearby grocery store with her late husband Guy from 1947 on. Betty also recalls that the Royal was strategically located on a big bend in Highway 90 coming into town, and that there were four service stations in the vicinity. "He (A.J.) got a lot of tourist business as a result," says Betty. And they – the tourists – didn't even have to budge from their cars if they didn't want to: curb service was a feature of the Royal.

Longtime Del Rio resident Max Stool, 75, recollects that "The business was well-run with a good staff." Although, Max continues, "A.J., himself, didn't spend much time at the restaurant. He preferred to drive around in his car and leave (his wife) Peggy to tend to the Royal."

Betty and Max both agree the Cafe's food was good. But then again, adds Betty, "Everything was good then. Going to a restaurant to eat was a treat. And you'd see a lot of people you knew because it (the Royal) was popular."

By the late 1950s, recalls Betty, the Royal's business was starting to decline. "They (A.J. and Peggy) weren't tending to business as much as they might have," is how Betty explains it. Things only got worse in the 1960s. A.J. closed the Royal Cafe in 1966. The building that housed it was eventually demolished. On the site today there is a Town & Country Convenience Store and Service Station.

ROYAL CAFE AND DRIVE-IN — On Highway 90 — DEL RIO, TEXAS

Intersection Highways to San Antonio, El Paso, Laredo, and Mexico

Circa 1950 Postcard View

Stebbins Grill
412 West Chestnut Street
Louisville, Kentucky

Some of the eateries included in WHERE HAVE YOU GONE, STARLIGHT CAFE? were decidedly more upscale than others. Stebbins Grill may just have been the most decidedly upscale of all. And while daughters are almost certain to be at least a little prejudiced, one cannot help but feel that George H. Stebbins' daughter (actually daughter-in-law, although she usually refers to her father-in-law as "Grandpa Stebbins") Wilma, 77, is telling nothing but the truth when she talks of the Stebbins Grill:

"The steaks, seafood and vegetables were always delicious, prepared to perfection, and the service as flawless as humanly possible. Grandpa Stebbins wouldn't allow it to be less. He carved all the steaks personally. Pre-packaged meats were unheard-of at Stebbins Grill. Desserts, with the exception of ice cream, were prepared each day by a wonderful lady whom we all knew as 'Miss Biddie.'

"The waiters, most of whom worked at Stebbins Grill for many years, were always polite and friendly. They dressed in white dinner jackets, black bow ties, pressed black trousers and highly polished black shoes. They always made you feel welcome and the service was the kind you only dream of today.

"Adorning each table was a spotless white tablecloth and napkins, condiments in silver or glass containers, and comfortable chairs that simply added to the feelings of elegance and gentility.

"As an example of Grandpa Stebbins' attention to and penchant for impeccable service, the butter was always served in fresh pats atop a small bowl of ice. Today, of course, you find it either in a small plastic container or wrapped in foil nestled against your baked potato, assuring that more of it runs down your fingers than gets on the potato or your dinner roll as you try to scrape it on to your butter knife, if you're fortunate enough to get a butter knife.

"Grandpa Stebbins' rationale for such good service was simple: He always said, 'People come to Stebbins Grill to dine, not just eat.'"

The roots of Stebbins Grill were more humble, going back to 1923 when George H. Stebbins, recently moved to Louisville from his native Michigan, opened Stebbins Cafeteria in the basement of a downtown insurance company building. A decade later, in 1933, George moved to the location pictured here…the location where people came to dine, not just eat.

And dine is exactly what people did. A luncheon menu still treasured by Wilma dates from June 5, 1937 (at Stebbins the menu was changed daily!) and lists Roast Spring Lamb for 45¢, Broiled Brook Trout for 85¢, a Boiled Half Maine Lobster for $1.00. All came with salad, hot rolls and butter, beverage, and a choice of two – out of a total of eight – vegetables. If you felt like splurging, dessert choices included strawberry shortcake (15¢), blackberry cobbler (15¢), and the one I know I'd have selected hands down, apricot pie (for all of 10¢).

George H. Stebbins retired from day-to-day operation of the restaurant he'd made famous in 1945, turning his attention instead to a new place he at first named the Swizzle Cafe, then Stebbins Steak House. He retired from the food business in 1965 and passed away at the age of 84 in 1974. His location at 412 West Chestnut Street has, in the years since Stebbins Grill, been occupied by various and sundry endeavors including Leo's Twinburger, Leo's Hideaway, Big Moe's Restaurant, and the New Orleans House. Since 1992 – looking not a bit as it did in its old postcard days – it has been occupied by a mod clothing and sports apparel shop called Soul Train.

STEBBINS GRILL   412 W. CHESTNUT STREET   LOUISVILLE 2, KENTUCKY

Circa 1940 Postcard View

Circa 1953 Postcard View

Steve's Restaurant
Route 301, North
Selma, North Carolina

Steve's Restaurant stood near the intersection of Highways 301 and 70, just over the Selma line from Smithfield (in the east-central section of the state, 30 miles southeast of Raleigh). "The fact that the building was standing at all," states local historian Doris R. Cannon, "made it a rarity." It seems that on March 7, 1942 an army munitions truck stalled in the immediate vicinity of the structure that would become Steve's, in an area called "Catch-Me-Eye" (a business district designed to catch the eye by way of an abundance of neon and brightly-colored buildings). An engine problem caused a stray spark to ignite the mass of explosives on board the truck. Suddenly, per Doris, "All of Catch-Me-Eye was under siege." As Doris further relates: "The blast left a 30-foot crater in the highway. Several deaths occurred and several buildings, including a substantial hotel, were destroyed. As far as 30 miles away, war-jittery citizens heard the explosion and thought sure that enemy bombs were being dropped on North Carolina." One man who operated a bar in the area, having come through the explosion unscathed, vowed to never again serve another alcoholic beverage. Or to ever again drink one, either.

Enter Steve's Restaurant ten years later, in 1952. Steve Loulas came to Selma specifically to open a restaurant. From whence he came nobody knows. He was just suddenly there, serving good old American food at prices that were far from extravagant. A newspaper ad from December of the restaurant's inaugural year offers a half a barbecue chicken for $1.25, seafood platters for $1.50, and choice steaks "Cooked To Your Order." Steve also wished one and all a Merry Christmas and a Happy New Year.

Steve's was not a smash success. By late 1954 it was closed. And Steve was gone. As Smithfield/Selma historian Margaret Lee puts it: "He didn't stay here very long."

There is, today, very little recall of Steve Loulas or his restaurant. Nor is there much recall of the building that housed his effort. A few people recall that it was utilized by a man named Shorty Parker – who sold insurance and fertilizer – for a while after Steve had vacated. But that's it. It is known that somewhere along the way the building was demolished. It had withstood the Blast of '42…but it couldn't withstand the march of "progress." On the site there is now a Revco Drug Store.

Sugar Loaf Cafe
301 East St. George Boulevard
St. George, Utah

When St. George (located in the extreme southwest corner of the Beehive State) celebrated the conclusion of World War II in 1945 there were exactly three restaurants in which to celebrate. Local businessman Don McDonald thought the town could support a fourth. In 1946 he leased a plot of ground and had the Sugar Loaf constructed. It was a smart move. As area historian Doug Adler explains: "St. George is on the direct route between Salt Lake City and Las Vegas, and in those days it was too long a trip to do in one day. St. George was a logical stopover. People would eat, maybe catch a movie, sleep."

After a dozen years at the helm Don McDonald sold the Sugar Loaf. The new owner was an entrepreneur named Sid Atkins. He kept the name "Sugar Loaf" – so called in honor of the red sandstone mountain range, part of which looks not unlike a loaf of bread, that served as a backdrop for the cafe – and featured what Doug refers to as "an American menu." That translated to "nothing international of any kind…just good homemade bread and pies and mainline stuff like stews, beef, and potatoes. And good portions." As far as atmosphere went, it was what Doug refers to as "low key." Plastic tablecloths, a record player with records playing. That sort of thing. Busy season was Memorial Day to Labor Day. A second busy period came in October, during hunting season.

The big story, though, was catering to the movie business. Sid, plus his brother Clayton and their father Rudger, bought a bus with a walk-in refrigerator and contracted with movie companies to supply on-location food to area filming sites. This was primarily in the late 1960s and early 1970s. But it was into the 1980s as well. The Atkins especially recall *The Electric Horseman,* a 1979 production starring Jane Fonda, Robert Redford, and Willie Nelson. They ought to: the film was on location nearby for a full three months. Some of the shooting was even done right in their parking lot. Doug recounts how Sid ran into Willie Nelson in the lot one day and "wondered who in the world he was. He (Willie) looked just like a transient."

In 1975 Sid and family moved operations to a newer, larger, and much pricier location across the street. They sold their original cafe – the one pictured here – to NAPA Auto Parts, who utilized it as a retail store/warehouse until early 1997. They then demolished it. On the site there is now a brand new NAPA superstore.

Sugar Loaf Cafe – St. George, Utah

Circa 1950 Postcard View

Circa 1940 Postcard View

Towers Cafe
325 East 7th St./Routes 67 & 71
Texarkana, Arkansas

It was known as "The Broadway of America." It was U.S. Route 67, the main highway (before Interstate 30 came along) between Dallas and Little Rock. And it was, in the words of Stuart Daniels of the Texarkana Chamber of Commerce, "a very dominant artery." Continues Mr. Daniels: "Highway 67, from a business point of view, was magic. All you had to do was open your doors and you were an instant success."

It was unto this magic thoroughfare that a man named Bernard Ghio opened the Towers Cafe in the late 1930s. Ghio and his manager, Tom Brown, weren't on the scene for long, however. Ghio sold to the husband/wife team of John and Mary Papageorge in mid-1941. The Papageorges continued the wide range of selections begun by Ghio and Brown. Among the dishes featured on an early menu are Old Style Fried Chicken (50¢), the Towers' Steak Plate (40¢), Lamb Chops (40¢), and Tenderloin of Trout (35¢). Another favorite was the Two States Special Sandwich, a blending of Arkansas Razorback Bacon and Selected Texas Beef. The price = 20¢. ("Worth 35¢ in either state," proclaimed the menu's copywriter!).

The Papageorges owned and operated the Towers until 1950. Recalls their daughter, Agnes Arnold: "My father was Greek; my mother Italian. Everybody in town knew everyone else. The Towers was a meeting place and, as time went by, my father and mother became known as 'Pop' and 'Mom'. Not only by all the young people but by the older ones as well." Agnes also recalls an incident that still gets her laughing: "One night, around 1944, a bunch of local boys decided to play a prank. They brought a greased pig into the restaurant and let it go. Talk about excitement! My dad was speaking so fast, and I wouldn't have been surprised if he were saying a cuss word or two. But I couldn't tell...he was speaking in Greek!"

What people mostly recall, not surprisingly, is the Towers' distinctive design. "It was eye-catching," says L.R. Maddox, 70. "It sure had a different shape," puts forth Rae McLean, 58. Rae used to go to the Towers with her father, who was a policeman ("on the Arkansas side," she makes quite clear.). "It was ahead of its time," sums up Texarkana (Texas) City Manager George Shackelford.

By the late 1940s the Papageorges began to feel the effects of fast food sprawl. It was not a good feeling. They sold the Towers in 1950.

The cafe with the distinctive design went through numerous proprietors – and themes – from 1950 to 1991. It was, in succession, a cafe, a steak house, a pizza parlor, a private club, a nightclub. The 50-plus year old building burned to the ground in early 1991. Nothing has since been built on its site. (Ed. note: for more on what's left of the Towers Cafe please see page 108.).

U.S. Grill
113 North Broadway/Highway 101
Santa Maria, California

One of the stories that always makes seventy-five year old Ethel Shiffrar smile when she remembers her dad is what I call "The George Story." It seems he – her dad – had two waiters named George. His solution: he called one of them "Big George" and one of them "Little George." It was not brilliant. But it was resourceful. And perhaps more than anything else, Mike Firfires – Ethel's dad and the U.S. Grill's dad, too – was resourceful.

Born to Greek parents in Turkey in 1886, Mike came to America at age 21, in 1907. His father had been a shoemaker and Mike at first followed more or less in the same footsteps, working in a shoe factory in Petaluma, California. His wife-to-be, Ethel Kimes, taught him to speak and read and write English. They were married in 1911. The couple lived first in San Diego; then Santa Barbara. It was while in Santa Barbara that Mike, as with so many Greek immigrants before him, went into the restaurant business. He became a waiter; then a cook. Eventually he opened a small cafe with a fellow Greek-American. In 1918 he took a giant step: he moved to Santa Maria (located just off the coast, 180 miles northwest of Los Angeles) and opened his very own restaurant. And since he was in America and since he was proud of it, he named it the U.S. Grill.

The Grill's first location was on East Main Street, but by 1927 Mike was doing so well he was able to afford larger space at 113 North Broadway, where it all happened, on the Coast Highway. Highway 101.

It was at the Highway 101 location – the one pictured here, with Mike standing tall in the entranceway – that Mike enjoyed his greatest success. According to Ethel, "The U.S. Grill was known up and down the central coast as one of the best places to eat." It being California, luminaries abounded. Famous folk known to have dined at the U.S. Grill include Tom Mix, Wallace Beery, Laurel and Hardy, Buck Jones, and the legendary Fatty Arbuckle. Another notable was William Randolph Hearst, who would stop in on his way to or from his estate at San Simeon. They all loved the Grill's juicy steaks and fresh-every-day seafood.

By 1944 Mike Firfires decided it was time to retire. He sold the U.S. Grill. Mike eventually died, in 1970, but the restaurant tradition he established at 113 North Broadway continues on. It's been the Santa Maria Grill (1946-1956), the Chew Cafe (1957-1975), the Bamboo Garden Restaurant (1976-1981). It is today – looking very little like it did in its old U.S. Grill days – the North China Chinese Restaurant.

Circa 1930 Postcard View

INTERIOR VIEW OF THE VICTORY CAFE, MATTOON, ILL.

THE BEST RESTAURANT IN THE BEST TOWN IN CENTRAL ILLINOIS   "WE SATISFY THE INNER MAN."

Circa 1935 Postcard View

Victory Cafe
1710 Broadway
Mattoon, Illinois

"The Victory Cafe wasn't a restaurant. It was an institution." So proclaims Bill Hamil, publisher of the Mattoon *Journal Gazette,* in summing up what the Victory meant to his hometown of Mattoon (located in east-central Illinois, roughly 80 miles southeast of the state capital, Springfield.).

Pete Sutter – the man who made the Victory Cafe happen – was born Peter Sotiropoulou in Aegeon, Greece in 1890. In 1903, at the youthful age of 13, he was packed up and sent off to America. He spoke no English, so he wore a tag that simply said his name and "St. Louis, Missouri." Arriving in St. Louis, where he had relatives, Pete began his restaurant career by working as a bus boy in a downtown hotel for $3.00 a week. Next came stints as waiter, assistant chef, and finally, in the Army during World War I, chef.

Following the War, Pete teamed up with a fellow Greek-American named John Katsinas to open a restaurant in Decatur, Illinois. A year later, in 1919, they moved to Mattoon and opened the Victory Cafe, first at 1814 Broadway and then, in 1923, at 1710 Broadway. Circa 1930 the partners split: John moved to Champaign; Pete held fast in Mattoon.

Bill Hamil gets *pretty* excited when he describes the Victory as it was at 1710 Broadway: "It had an octagonal tile floor, wooden booths with art deco–like lamps at the end of each one, and a long white marble counter with an equally long row of stools. It was," Bill again sums up, "a neat place." Bill gets *downright* excited when he describes the Victory's gastronomical treats and Pete's delight in "serving up great plates of 'Manhattan' sandwiches: tender beef served on Mattoon's own Sally Ann Bread and mounds of mashed potatoes – *real* potatoes – topped off with steaming brown gravy." Bill's recollections are from the 1940s but, he beams, "I can still taste them."

"Steaks," continues Bill, "were from the local Stydle packing house and melted in your mouth." And the mention of steaks reminds Bill of his Uncle Jesse. It seems Jesse liked to have some fun on a Saturday night and his idea of fun was to take his large black cocker spaniel, Wally, to the Victory. "He (Uncle Jesse) would always sit at the counter, order a steak and a hamburger. Jesse ate the hamburger…and Wally had the steak. The Victory's patrons loved it!" (Ed. note: you'd have to think that Wally did, too.).

In 1950, Pete suffered a cerebral hemorrhage while vacationing with his wife in Hot Springs, Arkansas. He was never the same again. Neither was the Victory. Pete sold the business in 1957 (and died in 1962.). His former cafe served for a while as a German restaurant; then a Chinese. Most recently the space has been occupied by a restaurant/nightclub called Images. As of my stay in Mattoon, in July 1997, it was vacant.

Warren's Dining Room and Restaurant
34 South Main Street
Bel Air, Maryland

There aren't many people in Bel Air (located 25 miles northeast of Baltimore on U.S. Route 1) who recall Warren's Dining Room and Restaurant anymore. But those few who do paint a mighty inviting portrait of it. Here's how a composite might read:

The first floor consisted of a confectionery shop and a lunchroom where simple and quick noontime meals were served. After several years the main dining room was moved to the second floor and was reached via a separate stairway from Main Street. When entering the restaurant in the summer you were greeted by lovely outdoor flower boxes in each window of the second floor.

Upstairs was a most attractive dining room with colorful window curtains, white tablecloths, good silverware, attractive plates, and tables decorated with fresh flowers.

The waitresses wore uniforms and were very attentive to guests. The whole atmosphere was conducive to fine dining.

It *does* sound inviting, doesn't it?

What would become Warren's, circa 1925, was founded as The Korner Konfectionery in 1920. The man who founded it, Ruskin Warren, chose his site well. Number 34 South Main was a solid brick building originally constructed in 1867. More important was where it was situated. As Marlene Magness of The Historical Society of Harford County explains: "The restaurant was well-located. It was on Court House Square, where it attracted many people connected with the court as well as lawyers who'd established their offices nearby." Being adjacent to the business district didn't hurt, either. When all was said and done,

however, it was Ruskin Warren's food that made his restaurant a winner. Seafood dishes such as oysters, scallops, and soft-shelled crabs were an especial treat.

People in Bel Air – as well as travelers on busy Highway U.S. 1, which ran right through town – not only liked Ruskin's food…they liked him and his outgoing and friendly manner. It hurt that much more, then, when Warren packed up his family and himself and moved away in 1932. He, not surprisingly, closed his restaurant in the process.

Ruskin's solid brick building has since housed the Court Square Restaurant, then Clark's Stationery. Since 1983 it's been home to Legg Mason, a stock brokerage firm. It's still solid brick. (Ed. note: for more on the building today please see page 114.)

WARREN'S DINING ROOM AND RESTAURANT,
"The Proprietor and his family eat there"   BELAIR,   -:-   MARYLAND.

Circa 1930 Postcard View

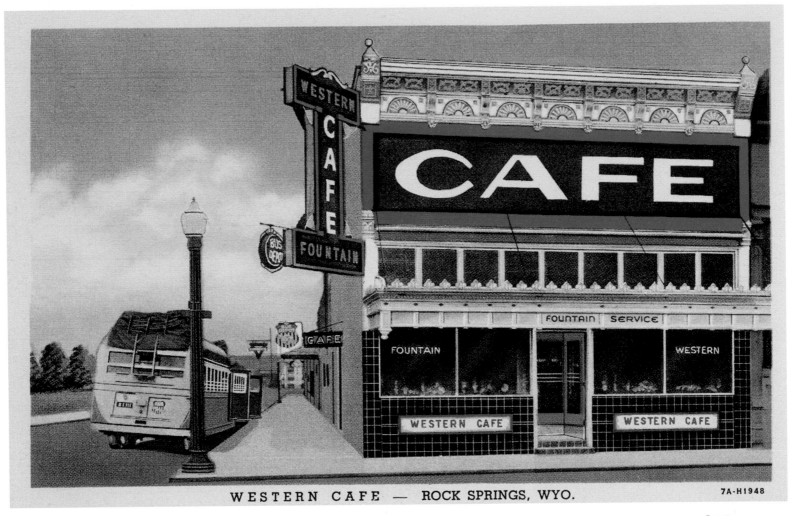

WESTERN CAFE — ROCK SPRINGS, WYO.

7A-H1948

Circa 1950 Postcard View

Western Cafe
403 North Front Street
Rock Springs, Wyoming

One of my favorite research finds was Joseph Oleffe. I came upon him while he was out for a stroll on a July Rock Springs afternoon. He looked to be the "right age," didn't appear to be in a rush, and was on the shady side of the street. The latter was a necessity: the temperature was over 100°, and the humidity wasn't very comforting, either. I showed him a copy of the view pictured here and inquired if he had any memories. "I used to wash dishes there, in 1942-1943," was his reply.

Joe was a teenager all those years ago, but the Western Cafe remains vivid in his mind. He recalls liking the owners and their food, especially their chicken and rice. That was his favorite. What Joe remembers most, though, is how much business the Western did. How crowded it was. "And I ought to know," he laughs: "I had to wash the dishes."

The building that became the Western Cafe earlier housed the Oxford Bar, where Butch Cassidy (who acquired his nickname from working for a butcher in Rock Springs: his real name was Leroy) reputedly hid out before taking off for South America. It later became the Vienna Cafe, a name that was then dropped as a protest against the Austro-Hungarian Empire during World War I. Rock Springs knew the good guys from the bad guys.

Southern Wyoming has a fairly sizable Chinese community, going back to earlier in this century when they worked in the area's coal mines. Foraging beneath the earth, however, didn't hold instant appeal for everyone. One such dissident was Tom Chum, who was proprietor of the Western from 1930 to 1935, and who set the standard for numerous Americans of Chinese descent in the Western's ensuing years.

While both Chinese and American dishes shared the menu, it's the American that people recall best. And people do recall. Leonard Merrell, who owns a furniture store around the corner from the Cafe's location, recollects "round stools with chrome edges and green upholstery in the center." Those stools will forever be ingrained in Leonard's mind for the best of reasons: as a kid he'd go in and spin them around and around. Roxana Brown, 74, had more weighty things to do than spin stools when she and her husband Grant frequented the Western in the early 1950s. "We'd have Denver omelettes," she beams. "They were so good." For Art Taucher, 81, it was the breaded veal sandwich that beckoned. Art and his pals would visit the Western after dances in the late 1930s. His favorite memory is how they'd tease Sammy (longtime proprietor Sam Wong): "We always had him recite the entire list of pies …and then order hot breaded veal sandwiches anyway. He'd always laugh at that."

The Western Cafe operated until 1968. Its building was then used, in order, as a shoe store, a children's clothing store, a small appliance outlet, and an arts and crafts supply store. It is now, and has been since the spring of 1995, a pool hall. (Ed. note: for more on the building today please see page 115.).

White Rose Diner
James Road/Routes 36 & 61
Hannibal, Missouri

Did Tom Sawyer or Huck Finn or Becky Thatcher ever enjoy a meal at the White Rose Diner? No. Nor did Mark Twain. But it appears as if most everyone else I talked with in Hannibal had somewhere along the way.

The White Rose opened for business in May of 1938. On Sunday, May 15th, to be exact. Mrs. Herbert J. (Louise) Engel was the proud proprietor. Her opening day ad in *The Hannibal Courier-Post* promised "Good, clean, home cooked food at popular prices." Featured in the ad was the diner's Special 65¢ Dinner: Green Beans, New Potatoes in Cream, Asparagus Vinaigrette, Beverage, Ice Cream, and your choice of Smothered Chicken and Dumplings, Prime Rib of Beef, a T-Bone Steak, or Fried Spring Chicken. All for 65¢. Sounds pretty popular to me.

As indicated by the postcard view included here, the White Rose was not what one would call spacious. When it opened on that Sunday in May in 1938, however, it was smaller still: only the door and the right-hand portion of the structure shown here were in existence. The entire left side was yet to happen. Ditto for the great HOME COOKING lettering. Louise wisely offered curb service to help alleviate the shortage of space.

What people remember about the White Rose, however, is not its curb service or its great HOME COOKING lettering. What they remember is the cooking itself. John Sherman's favorite was the chicken dinner. "It was the way they cooked it," he reminisces back to the late 1940s and early 1950s. Alvis L. Newsome, 70, had a fondness for the chicken, too. In fact, he'd have it – fried – most every day for lunch. "It was good. Very good," he notes with a smack of his lips. Then there's Bob Blanton, 68. Bob liked the homemade vegetable soup. Lastly is Forrest Taylor, 60. Forrest's usual was a hamburger or cheeseburger. Sometimes chili. "They had good food," he sums up, "and good coffee, too. It had good flavor."

Louise Engel owned and operated the White Rose until 1944 or so. Clifford Piper, proprietor of the next-door Piper's Skelly Fortified Gasoline Station, then took over. He made a name change, to Piper's White Rose Diner. Later still came Erma Glenn, then Fern Felter. Fern changed the eatery's name to Fern's Restaurant in 1964. Since 1993 the old diner – greatly enlarged and modernized ("uglified" would perhaps be a more appropriate term) beyond even a shadow of recognition – has been operating as a truck stop named Kathy B's.

Circa 1945 Postcard View

THE WINDHAM GRILL — WILLIMANTIC, CONNECTICUT   5A-H1985

Circa 1935 Postcard View

Windham Grill
585 Main Street/U.S. Route 6
Willimantic, Connecticut

The North Street Bakery had jelly or cream doughnuts – your choice – at 25¢ a dozen. Roast pork was 15¢ a pound at Noheimer's Market. Milevitz's Clothing Store listed men's overalls ("Good and Heavy") for 79¢ and work pants for $1.00. It was Saturday, November 21, 1931 in Willimantic, Connecticut. And it was Grand Opening Day at the Windham Grill.

With a slogan – Faultless Food For Fastidious Folks – that showed an obvious respect for alliteration, the eatery's ads proclaimed "The Windham Grill represents an investment of about $20,000, is one of the largest, most sanitary diners in Eastern Conn., in fact in the entire state. It will provide an eating place excelled by none with the best of food, properly cooked and served, at a minimum price." The seating capacity was given as 60, with 40 of it via tables and 20 via counter stools. The diner's ad closed by stating "There are nicely appointed rest rooms for men and women and above all plenty of parking space."

The Windham Grill was the crowning glory of Steve Chontos. No stranger to Willimantic (in eastern Connecticut, 20 miles from Hartford), Chontos had earlier, from 1927 to 1930, operated a lunch wagon on the future site of his Grill. Before that he'd run an eatery at 451 Main. He would run the Windham Grill (with a name change to the Windham Diner in 1951) until he retired and moved to Vermont in 1958.

His creation is fondly remembered. Francis Wright, 82, terms it "classy." Francis admits to Willimantic having had a number of "greasy spoons." But the Windham wasn't one of them, he makes perfectly clear. "It was a cut above that." Jean Bouffard, 70, remembers the Windham as "a beautiful diner…with all chrome inside." (Claire Meikle, 71, worked at the Grill as a waitress in the mid-1940s and well recalls all the chrome and stainless steel: "There was a young girl who polished it. Every day. She did it real speedy. So speedy," Claire chuckles, "that it almost made you tired watching her.") Jean's husband Al has better recall of the food than the decor: "The food was always good. You could go in there and get ham and eggs or pancakes and bacon. The whole works. Whatever you wanted." And, he smiles at Jean, "I used to eat out a lot. I was single then."

My favorite memory comes from Ruth Ridgeway, 87, who recalls when her late husband Benton worked for the Windham National Bank: "Every year the bank examiners would come and everyone at the bank would have to stay around until all the examining was done, and then they'd all go out to dinner." Well, one year, around 1950, one of the employees, Willard "Pinky" Olds, a real practical joker, suggested the Windham Grill for dinner. "And he led the assembled group there and through the front door…and then into the men's room." Laughs Ruth: "They all pretended to be horrified, but they were really amused. It was Willard's little joke."

Steve Chontos sold to new proprietor Peter Wojnar in 1958. It was then, from 1961 to 1970, George Haddad's turn to be owner/operator. Urban Development came to downtown Willimantic in the early 1970s, with the usual, almost predictable, results: the Windham and the area around it were leveled. On the former diner's site there is now a municipal parking lot. (Ed. note: on the address side of the postcard shown here the following is printed: "More than 300,000 patrons served in 1934, requiring six tons of hamburg; over 200,000 cups of coffee; 5 1/2 tons of sugar; 96,000 eggs; etc. The Grill is *never closed*.").

Y Barbeque
Rochester & East Savannah Rds./Jct. Routes 71 & 169
St. Joseph, Missouri

The postcard view featured here is a bit of a puzzler. First, "Eads For Eats" would certainly imply that the restaurant shown in the view was called "Eads." It wasn't. Second, the positioning of the structures in the view bears little resemblance to reality. More on that later.

What was known as the Y Barbeque was opened for business by a man named E. Cook Eads in 1932. He called it "Y" because it was located at the intersection (the "Y") of two major roads. E. Cook added here and added there. Cabins and a large dance floor resulted. But it was always his food for which Mr. Eads was most famous. Ninety-year old Harold M. Slater, a resident of St. Joe almost his entire long life, recalls it well: "The food was excellent. Tourism was still rather light in the 1930s and the place relied on St. Joseph customers mostly." As Harold continues: "The restaurant specialized in hearty meals and sandwiches. Nothing gourmet! It had the usual roast beef, ham, and hamburger meals and sandwiches, all at very reasonable prices. A good barbeque rib sandwich cost 20¢ or 25¢. With French fries."

Fritz Hirter, a relative youngster at age 78, has memories, too. "Cook Eads was a big, proud fellow and he was friendly. Of course," adds Fritz, "he had to be. He was wanting business and there were two other barbeque places close by."

In or around 1943 the Y Barbeque (but not the cabins) burned down. Cook Eads did not rebuild. He instead went into the manufacture of garage doors. The "Y" was just too good a location, however, to sit idle. By 1945 a new, but far less spacious, Y Barbeque was in operation, with a man named William Turner its proprietor. Numerous other proprietors – and names – followed. There was Hall's Y Cafe, Sportsman Cafe, Gussy's Barbeque, the Maid Rite Restaurant. Later came Richardson & Son's Realty and, finally, the present occupant, Eisenburg's One-Stop Vacuum Shop.

Before we leave St. Joe, however, it's interesting to note the lengths the postcard artist assigned to the Y went to to make it, in his or her opinion, look more appealing. He/she switched most everything around, moving whole buildings in the process! Harold and Fritz had suggested that something seemed wrong with the view as shown here. Olive Martin, 76, who with her late husband Cleo owned and operated the next-door "cabins" (they were actually much more like motel units) for 29 years, explained precisely why: in real life the cabins/motel units were to the right – not the left – of the restaurant. Plus the cabins/motel units were facing the other way. What is pictured on the postcard, in other words, is the rear of the units. The artist flip-flopped the units around to present a more attractive appearance. Pretty amazing. But very true. (Ed. note: for more on the buildings of today please see page 108.).

"EADS FOR EATS"
Fine Foods at Reasonable Prices

PEACOCK LOUNGE

E. C. EADS Prop.

CABINS
Air-conditioned & Heated

FOR EATS

CABINS
AIR CONDITIONED

CABINS
AIR CONDITIONED

CABINS

FOR EATS

NORTH JUNCTION U. S. 71 AND 169 -- ST. JOSEPH, MISSOURI

7A H534

Circa 1940 Postcard View

Here's Catherine and I and our rented Buick Skylark. We named her "Starlight."

Part II: A Closer Look

From my abode in Portland, Maine to Santa Maria, California and back again is roughly 6,300 miles. I did it in 14,133.

Actually, I could possibly have done it in zero. From the very beginning of January to late June of 1997 I corresponded – by way of the telephone and the mails – with local historians, librarians, and government officials in each of the book's 40 "Target Towns." It netted an impressive body of information. But it wasn't enough. For the Western Cafe, in Rock Springs, Wyoming, for example, I had nothing. Zip. For the White Rose Diner, of Hannibal, Missouri fame, I had some information but it was suspect. My contact had informed me that his research showed a starting date of 1949. Yet my White Rose postcard was postmarked 1940. Something seemed amiss. Much more important, however, was the need for "hands on." To verify what information I did have. To fill in the gaps where I didn't have. And to actually visit and see and touch each of the target structures, regardless of how much or how little remained of each.

The open road beckoned.

I set out with my wife Catherine. "I" became "we." We departed Maine bright and early on June 22nd in a rented 1997 Buick Skylark. With unlimited mileage. It was a good thing: before we returned 63 days later we had zigged and zagged those 14,133 miles. The car's odometer read 1772 miles when we set out; 15,905 when we returned. We had taken a new car and made it old.

We went through 39 states, virtually all on two-lane or old major roads. We ate in mom and pop cafes and grills and diners. We stayed in non-chain motels. We talked with scores and scores of local history aficionados, local public employees, local old-timers, and just plain local wonderful people.

We had a ball.

"None of Them"

When we returned home, armed with multitudinous facts, stories, and photos, a friend asked "How many of them (the "targets") are the same?" I gave the only answer I could: "None of them." Time had taken a heavy toll.

Still, over half of our targets remained in existence in one form or another. We did our best to capture 18 of them on film. Of those we skipped, some were because the weather was not conducive to any kind of decent photography; others because they simply didn't "say" anything to us.

The 18 are arranged in a more-or-less "how much remains" order. First comes "Just a Trace," then "Different Building/Same Theme," followed by "In There Somewhere," etc. Of course, there were crossover categories. Plus there's the fact that we're human and some people touched us more than others…with the result their structure may have more space than it otherwise would. The point: don't take the sequence too seriously.

**Route 6 sign,
Holyoke, Colorado**

**Route 66 sign,
somewhere south of Oatman, Arizona**

Apart from taking a photo here or there, only after our "Journey of a Lifetime" was over did we take much stock of what routes our targets had been on. Or how many miles we had driven on this highway or that highway. When we did do a little tallying we found that storied Chicago–to–Los Angeles Route 66 was the highway of choice for the greatest number (five) of our targets, while it was U.S. Route 6 (which wends its way across America from Cape Cod to California) on which we drove far and away the most (over 650 miles: across northern Pennsylvania, southern Nebraska, northeastern Colorado, western Utah, and, much later, eastern Connecticut, Rhode Island, and southeastern Massachusetts.). You might say we got our kicks on Route 6/66!

As we made our way across America and back people we'd meet would ask us if we were on our way to Yellowstone. Or Las Vegas. Or the Grand Canyon. And we'd say no. That we were on our way to Kokomo. Or Boonville. Or Del Rio.

And we were.

Y Barbeque, St. Joseph, Missouri

If you look at the circa 1940 view of the Y Barbeque on page 102 you can't help but notice the huge "Y" positioned to the right. Actually, that positioning was yet another example of postcard artist license: the "Y" was actually atop a self-standing support that was separate and apart from the main – i.e. restaurant – building. (Separate and apart enough to escape destruction when the main building burned down circa 1943.). It today stands, harking not barbeque or cabins, but tax preparation and hair styling.

Towers Cafe, Texarkana, Arkansas

The Towers has experienced a most gruesome, even eerie, fate. After the fire that destroyed it in 1991, its remains consist of only its front steps and the tile floor marking its distinctive shape. Fried Chicken and K-C Steaks have been replaced by rubble and weeds.

Madison Diner, Mt. Holly, New Jersey

Here's Madison Diner Number 2…not exactly the sparkling gem that Madison Diner Number 1 (page 62) was. And, in all our in-person Top 40 research, this was the one establishment where we were not greeted as warmly as we might've been. As soon as the manager deduced we were there to chew the fat rather than eat, he lost interest in us. Then, even though we'd clearly explained our "mission," he got visibly upset when we started taking photographs. We concluded that southern – New Jersey – hospitality isn't always all it's cracked up to be.

Pilot Cafe, Salt Lake City, Utah

"It's been changed over," as employee Shirley Newman phrased it when we showed her our postcard view (page 77) of the Pilot in its "good old days." By that, Shirley, who's worked at the Pilot and its successors for 30 years, meant that the place today doesn't look much at all like it used to. She's right. But at least it's up and running and – as Club Shakers – serving pretty much the same role it always has: providing food, drink, and a lively dance floor. "It still attracts a neighborhood crowd, too," adds Shirley.

Cronk's Cafe, Denison, Iowa

The Cronk's you see here bears no resemblance to the Cronk's you see on page 30. That's because it's been enlarged and modernized several times. Present proprietor Eric Skoog assured us that the page 30 structure still stands intact within this new/enlarged edition. In spite of Eric's best efforts, however, we couldn't pick it out. That frustration aside, we enjoyed his guided tour; especially the collection of vintage Cronk's photos and memorabilia on display in the barroom.

Hick's Drive-In, Louisville, Kentucky

There's little to add to the Hick's/Jerry's story. We spoke with a number of long-standing customers who all agreed the place sure looked different when it was Hick's. The most "fun" was trying to get a decent photo. U.S. Route 31W – the Dixie Highway – is a busy, busy four-laner. Just getting across it – and back – to obtain the angle we wanted was a feat unto itself.

Court Cafe, Albuquerque, New Mexico

We had been told by several people that the Court Cafe was demolished many moons ago. So when we came upon the 4th Street Cafe at the Court's old address we couldn't help but believe it was a newcomer to the neighborhood. Then we met Pete Rallis, the 4th Street's proprietor, and he said, "Nope. Even though it looks very different it's the same building." He told us how older folks stop by ("They always seem to come at lunchtime when I'm really busy.") and tell him all about eating there years ago when it was the Court. How he's found 50-60 year-old newspapers hidden here and there. And, most of all, how, in 1996, he found a Court Cafe serving platter in the basement. "I found it under a bunch of boxes," he says. "I got pretty excited." (Ed. note: so did we. Here's Pete and the platter.).

George's, Cardiff by the Sea, California

We ate at exactly one chain/franchise restaurant on our entire 63-day jaunt. This was it. The Cardiff by the Sea Chart House. The "son" of George's. Expecting nothing, we were pleasantly surprised. The view of the Pacific was magnificent, the meal more than adequate, and, biggest surprise of all, our waiter knew all about George's. He told us that the beach immediately to the left of the restaurant is still often called "George's Beach." And he aimed us in the direction of the balcony and a wonderful large old black and white photo: there's George's and the entire staff standing tall sixty-five or so years ago. We liked it a lot.

Baker's Cafe, Afton, Oklahoma

It's time for the "Looks the Same (More or Less)" category. Flip back to pages 21, 61, 65, and 74 and you'll see what we mean. It was a favorite category for us: finding each place intact was like finding an old friend intact. And, since there *is* a fair similarity between then and now, you'd think we'd have had no difficulty in tracking each down. With the Marilorn and Phil's we didn't. But with Baker's and the Kentland we sure did. In Afton people kept pointing us toward the Route 66 Cafe. "That's the old Baker's Cafe," they'd say. But we didn't think so. Finally a woman in a local antique center suggested the daycare center. Our search was over.

In Kentland we knew our "target" was on Route 41 and had become a pizza parlor. We easily found Route 41. And we easily found a pizza parlor. Except it was newish. And ugly. We hoped the K.C. had met a better fate. And it had! We asked around and discovered that the State of Indiana, some years back, had moved Highway 41 a block east. We rounded the corner to old 41…and found the K.C., and found it looking almost identical to its postcard view. In fact, bring back the cars, the signs, and the green Spanish tile…and it is the postcard view.

Kentland Cafe, Kentland, Indiana

Marilorn Barbeque, Waverly, New York

When we found the Marilorn we also found Kay Onofre, who grew up across the street and whose family now owns the former barbeque and drive-in. She recalled how busy the Marilorn would be...and how, back in the early 1960s, she'd sit and watch people pull up in all kinds of different cars. "It was neat," she says with a flourish. Kay's favorite memory, though, is of her family's beagle, Meggy, and how Meggy would "patronize" the Marilorn, sitting up and begging for food. "What was her favorite?," we asked. "Was it the Texas hots or the barbeque with the secret sauce or something else?" Laughed Kay: "She wasn't fussy."

Phil's Restaurant, Elkins, West Virginia

It took many hours for it to cease being overcast the day we were in Elkins. But the wait was worth it: the old cafe's sleek facade looks so much better in the sun than it does in the rain.

Casa Linda Cafe, Kingman, Arizona

What used to be the Casa Linda (page 26) is now a surveying firm named CSNA. What used to be its address, East Front Street/Route 66, is now Andy Devine Avenue/Route 66. The rotund and raspy-voiced sidekick star of something like 400 movies grew up in Kingman, graduated from Kingman High, went on to national fame. He gained his "own" street in 1955 as a part of being honored on the "This Is Your Life" television show.

Warren's Dining Room, Bel Air, Maryland

"If the window boxes and shutters were still there," noted Catherine, "it would look exactly the same (as in its postcard view.)." There's no doubt the building that once housed Warren's and today houses Legg Mason is still a beauty, a credit to Bel Air. And ask Legg Mason branch manager Don Lomax to tell you about the folks who come by and want to talk about the structure's "good old days." Better yet, ask Don to show you the vintage Warren's postcard – different from the one on page 94 – that's nicely matted and framed and hanging in his office. It's a beauty, too.

Western Cafe, Rock Springs, Wyoming

"Oh, yeah, I have one of those myself," commented Darry Romsa when we showed him a copy of the postcard pictured on page 97. Darry is the proprietor of the Treasure Chest, the pool hall that now occupies the former cafe's building. He went on to tell us that people still come in – albeit occasionally – and say "I remember when I was a kid and this was a cafe."

The Frank's of yesterday. (Compare with page 45: it doesn't look quite as inviting as it used to.).

Sign advertising the Frank's of today.

Three generations of Tiliceks: Frank, Jr., Rosine, Frank, III. That's the top of a portrait of Frank, Sr. in the background.

Frank's Restaurant, Schulenburg, Texas

We arrived in Schulenburg on a wild day. It was a Sunday, and it was the final day of the 20th annual Schulenburg Festival and Rodeo, featuring everything from a chili cook-off and a softball tournament to a parade and "Nashville Recording Artist David Ball." It seemed as if everybody in south Texas was there and it seemed as if they were all congregating at Frank's. (The new Frank's, of course. It was pretty lonely at the old Frank's.). Still, after we traveled down Highway 77 and took a half a roll of photos of the old stand, our contact, Shirley Tilicek, rounded up longtime proprietors Rosine (Tilicek) and Frank, Jr. (also Tilicek) and somehow found a place for us to talk amidst the bedlam. Rosine was great. So was Frank, Jr. Some of their memories – and, between the two of them, we're talking 113 years of memories of Frank's! – are presented on page 44.

The Frank's of today.

Sign in the
Nu-Griddle's
parking lot.

Mazie and some of her memorabilia. The jukebox is new...the
selections are old.

Griddle Cafe, Plainview, Texas

Walking into the Nu-Griddle (the structure
that replaced the "old" Griddle) is not
unlike strolling back in time to the 1958
Senior Prom. There are records (45s, of
course) strung around the walls, and
posters of Elvis, Roy Orbison, Marilyn,
Buddy Holly & the Crickets (the pride of
nearby Lubbock), James Dean, and more.
Best of all is the jukebox. There's such '50s
classics as "Tutti-Frutti," "Sweet Little Sixteen," "What's
Your Name?" "Donna," and both of this author's all-time top
favorites: "Ain't It A Shame" by Fats Domino, and "I'll
Remember (In The Still Of The Night)" by the Five Satins.
They don't get any better than that! You can make your
selections from your booth, too. Just like 1958. It's all the
creation of present-day proprietor, Mazie McCarty. When
you talk with Mazie, who's 56, she points to her head and
says "I'm still a teenager up here." She could just as easily
be pointing to her heart.

A Plainview panorama: the Nu-Griddle on a clear 1997 summer's day.

One Spot Cafe, Salina, Kansas

The Trails End of today bears a very definite resemblance to the One Spot of yesterday. Check the roofline, windows, and entranceway in the photo shown here versus the postcard view on page 69. It's not identical by any means. But it's reasonably close…a result of the structure's not having been overly "modernized" through the years.

Of perhaps more importance: the Trails End is a "happy" place. New proprietor – she took over in August of 1996 – Debbie Werber is obviously enjoying herself. So, too, are her employees and her customers. Says Debbie: "I'm having fun. They (the patrons) all come in and feel comfortable. That makes me feel good. I have excellent employees. They keep everything

jumping." They sure do. The landmark eatery was alive with warmth the day we were there. Good food abounded, too. We had a homemade cinnamon roll – one of Debbie's house specialties – that was so huge that Catherine described it as "a cake." Other specialties included pan fried chicken, chicken fried steak, and chicken and noodles (homemade noodles) over mashed potatoes. (No, we did not try them all!). (Ed. note: as this section of the book was being written, four months later in November, we called Debbie and asked if she were still having fun. Her answer: an unequivocal "Yes, I am…great people; good atmosphere; never a dull moment.").

The cooking staff takes a break: from left to right, Suzanne Burton (Debbie's daughter), Debbie, Darlene Thomas.

Part III: A Tribute To Today

This last section of WHERE HAVE YOU GONE, STARLIGHT CAFE? came to be via the process of evolution. For the first week of our journey we chose where we ate based upon nothing more momentous than hunger and convenience. We were hungry. We looked for a place. As long as that place wasn't a franchise or part of a chain or too upscale…it was ok. We ate.

Then, on the eighth day, we discovered the plate lunch. We were traveling through Paris (Illinois!), on our way to Mattoon, when we came upon a packed parking lot in front of B & J's, a nondescript cafe off the court house square. We found it to be packed for good reason: $4.00 entitled you to a meat dish and your choice of any three vegetables/potatoes, plus dessert and coffee. All good portions. All good food.

We soon learned that the plate – very full plate – lunch is no stranger to most of mid- and southern America. But it was new to us. We were enamored.

For the next two weeks we began to be more selective, which translated to keeping a steady lookout for plate lunch possibilities as we made our way – and ate our way – across the midwest. It was not until our 21st day, however, that we took our first photo of anything that dealt with present-day eateries. And it was hardly an earth-shattering photo: a time-worn sign heralding the Main Street Cafe in Laddonia, Missouri. Our juices, though, were obviously stirred: the very next day we found ourselves interviewing and taking photos of Herbert and Virginia Flo Willard, proud proprietors of Bright's Grill on Highway 54 in Fort Scott, Kansas. They clearly enjoyed it. So did we.

Thus was born Part III. We were, admittedly, a little slow on the draw. It had taken us fully three weeks, but the light of realization finally dawned upon us: there are still, very thankfully, some pretty special locally owned/ locally operated restaurants dishing out some great meals all across the length and breadth of America.

We again sharpened our "selection factors." As before, there would be no franchises or chains. Who needs monotony? No franchise or chain wannabes, either. No sports bars. No drive-thrus. No retro. Places with names like "Joe's" or "Barb's" got top billing over places with names like "Elegant Armadillo," or "Peaches and Pumpkins." We discovered that the presence of pick-ups was a good sign. Most of all, though, we found that we enjoyed places that were "real," and that had some age to them. From the Golden Era, even. Age builds character. Lastly, we found ourselves partial to the word "cafe."

These next 20 pages, then, say "thanks" to some of the many present-day cafe proprietors and employees who brightened the long spaces between our Top 40 targets. And who gave us hope that – just down the road aways – the Starlight Cafe lives on.

Bright's Grill, Fort Scott, Kansas

Herbert and Virginia Flo Willard took over ownership of Bright's Grill (also known as Bright's Grille & Shake) in 1971. Herbert was constantly being laid off from his job as a toolmaker in the aerospace industry in Wichita. Result: when the chance to buy a restaurant and return to their old stomping grounds in western Missouri/eastern Kansas (where Fort Scott is located) came along, it seemed mighty appealing.

Twenty-six years later the Willards are still at it. Except now they're open all year. Bright's, named for an earlier owner, was originally built in 1957 as a drive-in, and was open "during the season" only. But, noted Virginia Flo, closing during the off season put people out of work. So the Willards added on and went year 'round.

Now 78 and 74, the Willards have no immediate plans to retire. As Virginia Flo reflects: "Sometimes it's real hard (the day-in/day-out operation of the Grill) but we've met some real nice people."

P.S. One thing we especially liked at Bright's was that, with any lunch or dinner meal, ice cream was free upon request. We requested.

Virginia Flo and Herbert Willard smile for the camera. Virginia was afraid her hair wouldn't look good because it would look white. We told her it would look great. And it does.

Employee Michella Sullivan ("I'm the first and only female employee here in 75 years.") and employee/manager Bob Spreier before the noontime hoards began to arrive.

The Cozy Inn was slated to be demolished in 1987 as part of a Spruce-Up Downtown project. But the patrons revolted; started a "Save The Cozy" campaign; rounded up over 7,000 signatures. The city changed its mind.

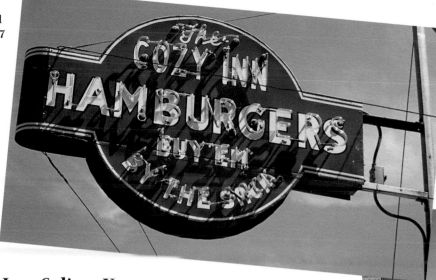

Cozy Inn, Salina, Kansas

It would be difficult for us to not like Salina. In the morning of the day we were there we went to – and definitely enjoyed – the One Spot/Trails End (see pages 99-100). Then, on our way through town, we discovered the Cozy Inn. It's a duo that would be tough to top. Anywhere.

The Cozy Inn goes back – way back – to 1922. That's the year a young man named Bob Kinkel set up shop on a side street in downtown Salina selling nickel hamburgers. These were not just any old nickel hamburgers, however: they came complete with ground-up onion and pickle slices. Mustard and/or ketchup was optional. You bought them "by the sack."

Seventy-five years later not much has changed but the price. "Cozies" – as they're affectionately called – sell for 55¢ each. Mustard and/or ketchup is optional. You buy them "by the sack."

And, as noon approached, we saw it happen. People started to come in. From seemingly everywhere. The tiny – six stools, all original – Cozy began to feel like Times Square. Some people ordered five to go. Some ten. One customer ordered an even dozen (two sacks of six). No one ordered one.

We liked Salina.

After a slow start, Michella turned into a regular cutup. As we were leaving she asked if her picture would be in the book. Our answer: "Yes, if it (the picture) turns out ok." Her answer: "Heck, it isn't a book if I'm not in it."

West 6th Street, Concordia, Kansas, July 16, 1997

Kountry Kitchen Cafe, Concordia, Kansas

Let's face it, West 6th Street is not a zingy-sounding
name. But in Concordia, Kansas (located in the north-
central part of the state) it's the main street and it's
like a walk back in time. First, there's the 1907
National Historic landmark Brown Grand Theatre at
310 West 6th. Then there's Lester's Sweet Shop
(Quick, when's the last time you heard the term
"Sweet Shop"?) at 210 West 6th. And then there's
"The Sign:" the marvelous old Kountry Kitchen Cafe
neon, which calls 217 West 6th home, that would be a
credit to any main street. Not everyone agrees,
though. "People sometimes tell me I ought to get a
new sign," says proprietress Aleta Ellis. Fortunately,
Aleta disagrees. "I like that sign," says she with conviction. "I think it's neat. Plus," she adds, "I think it
really attracts people." Aleta went on to tell us that, if
the same sign were put up today, it would have to be
flush with the building. New ordinances require it.
Because "The Sign" goes back to the 1950s, however,
it falls under old ordinances that allow it to be the
way it is. Thank goodness for old ordinances.

Across Nebraska, Colorado, Wyoming, and Utah, Too

Across southern Nebraska, northeastern Colorado, southern Wyoming, and north and central Utah we drove 1,000 miles without any appreciable success finding places that met our "standards." In Palisade, Nebraska we ate at McHenry's Palisade Cafe, just off U.S. Highway 6, and enjoyed a hefty-portion chicken fried steak. Palisade, last stop before mountain time, is not a big town. Its welcome sign boasts a population of 381. And its laundromat has one washer and one dryer. The weather, unfortunately, did not lend itself to picture-taking. Ditto with the City Cafe, in Ft. Morgan, Colorado, where we partook of breakfast on July 18th.

There were several others, too. Often, though, they were closed. We discovered that a fairly high percentage of our kind of place opened at 5:00 (or 6:00) AM and closed at 2PM. Arrive after 2:00 and you're on your own. We felt especially cheated re the Busy Bee, in Kemmerer, Wyoming (home of J.C. Penney's first store), and the Snappy Service Cafe (love that name!) in Ogden, Utah. Next time, we told ourselves.

Sign on State Highway 14 in the High Plains, Stoneham, Colorado

Top's City Cafe, Delta, Utah

In Delta ("The Place to Stay and Play") we lucked out: it was late
Sunday afternoon and yet our number one pick for dinner – Top's City
Cafe – was still open. But running low on provisions. "It's been one busy
weekend," announced waitress Jeannette Jones as soon as we walked in
and sat down. "Tomorrow we'll get restocked." We had to "settle" for
the last helping of Southern Fried Chicken (complete with beans, salad
bar, huge dinner roll, and mashed potatoes with gravy), and a Ribeye
(complete with same). Best of all, though, was the pie. It turns out that
Top's City   named for owner Peggy
Topham – is locally renowned for its homemade pies. Again, though, the busy weekend had taken its toll: Top's was down to
two choices – pineapple and pecan – from
their usual ten. We went with the pineapple and had no regrets.

**Smiling waitresses Cathy
Blankenship, left, and
Jeannette Jones**

Burro Bend Cafe, Ocotillo Wells, California

Probably the most amazing thing about the Burro Bend Cafe, located on Highway 78 in the extreme southern part of the state, is that it's there at all. There sure isn't much else in the way of buildings in the vicinity.

"It used to be a one-room house and the owner would serve meals out the front door," present-day co-proprietor (with husband Steve) Mary Murray told us. The section pictured here was added in 1938. Mary also told us that the Burro Bend's busy season is during the winter when the surrounding Anza-Borrego Desert comes alive with off-road vehicles. "During the summer, when it's 128°," she laughed, "no one wants to ride."

Frontier Cafe, Truxton, Arizona

From Kingman to Seligman (both located in Arizona's northwestern quadrant) is a quick 50-minute jump on today's Interstate 40. We chose, instead, to take yesterday's route, old 66, which loops north through almost-forgotten towns named Hackberry, Valentine, and Peach Springs. There's Truxton, too: home to a fair supply of seen-better-days buildings and one of our favorite signs, painted large and bold on the highway side of the Frontier Cafe. We stopped and asked manager Mildred Barker about it. "Do," we asked, "a lot of people tell you what a beautiful sign you have?" "No," she replied, "but a lot of people do take pictures of it."

Joe & Aggie's Cafe, Holbrook, Arizona

To travel through the southwest and not partake of Mexican-American fare would be like traveling through Bavaria and not partaking of beer. We've never been to Bavaria. But we've been to the southwest. We partook. One of our favorite spots, both for its food and its beauty, was Joe & Aggie's, on old Route 66 in Holbrook (in eastern Arizona). Originally opened as the Cactus Cafe in 1945, Joe & Aggie's became Joe & Aggie's when it was purchased by Joe and Aggie Montano in 1956. The tacos are especially wonderful. So are the murals, done by Holbrook artist Severo Barella, that adorn the restaurant's exterior walls. The front artwork was finished in 1978; the side in early 1997.

The side wall mural pays tribute to Highway 66 ("The Mother Road") and some of the major towns and cities along its route. Places like Albuquerque and Tulsa and St. Louis. Severo had a little trouble with the last one, though. When we inquired of present-day proprietor Alice Gallegos (she's Joe and Aggie's daughter) about it, she laughed. "He's a great painter...but you have to write things down. He does misspell things."

Evett's Cafe & Fountain, Magdalena, New Mexico

At Evett's you get a museum with your meal. Almost everywhere you look, from the 1950s' eight-stool soda fountain to the impressive display of old radios and cash registers to the pink walls embellished with Nesbitt Orange signs from a distant time, there's worthy stuff. It befits a building that has been a Highway 60/Main Street centerpiece in Magdalena (located in west-central New Mexico; elevation 6,548 feet) for 90 or so years. Built for use as a bank in the early years of the century, the handsome structure became a drug store/soda fountain in 1953; a cafe/soda fountain in 1988.

Texas Barbecue

Texans take their barbecue seriously. And so did we the five days and five nights – and 1350 miles – we spent traversing the Lone Star State. We even learned a thing or two as we went along.

Sign, Highway 21, Crockett, Texas

Pete's Bar-B-Que and Bait Stand, Castroville, Texas

Don't look for anyone named "Pete" at Pete's Bar-B-Que & Bait Stand on Route 90 West in Castroville. Ask, instead, for Rick Martinez. He's the man. "It's all in the pit," he told us when we asked the secret to barbecue. Rick's main pit (he has four of them) is a converted propane storage tank. "It's my best pit," he beams. His brisket of beef sandwiches, his best seller "by a long shot," are testimony to that.

Tyrone's BBQ & Catfish, Nacogdoches, Texas

"It's a little bit the meat and a little bit the sauce," said Tyrone Cartwright, proprietor of Tyrone's BBQ & Catfish on Routes 7 and 21 in Nacogdoches, when we asked the secret to barbecue. Tyrone was only in his second month when we stopped by, but based on our taste buds (his pork ribs and home-made sweet potato pie went down real easy) he was off to a good start.

H-Bar-C Pit Bar-B-Q, Brownfield, Texas

It's almost impossible to miss the "Eat Here!" sign that stands out-side the H-Bar-C on Highways 62 and 82 in Brownfield. It made us laugh. And it made us stop. We were glad we did, too, because then we got to meet Bonnie Lowe, the H-Bar-C's spirited 81-year old official cashier and unofficial greeter. She told us the sign was the brainchild of her daughter (co-proprietor Sue Cottrell) and that it had garnered lots of publicity. Mostly, though, she chuckled her way through the telling of what is obviously her favorite tale in the H-Bar-C's 19 years of operation. It seems that back in 1982 Sue had to go into the hospital; so she hung up a "Closed Due to Illness" sign. That, coupled with the "Eat Here! Even If" sign, really "took people aback," giggled Bonnie.

Sign, Top's City Cafe, Delta, Utah

So here they are. Our "Top Twelve." Our "Delicious Dozen." Presented – how else? – in time-honored countdown sequence:

Rating	Varietal	Place of Purchase
12	Sweet Potato	Frankie's Hertford Cafe, Hertford, North Carolina
11	Butterscotch Cream	Pioneer Cafe, Marshall, Missouri
10	Date Nut Cream	Stratford Inn, Danville, Virginia
9	Buttermilk	Lost Maples Cafe, Utopia, Texas
8	Key Lime	Coach-n-Four, Crestview, Florida
7	Pineapple	Top's City Cafe, Delta, Utah
6	Sweet Potato	Tyrone's BBQ & Catfish, Nacogdoches, Texas
5	Pecan	VFW Post #6735, Mt. Storm, West Virginia
4	Coconut Cream	Grammy's Kitchen, Charles Town, West Virginia
3	Pineapple Cream	Nu-Griddle Cafe, Plainview, Texas
2	Appleberry	Farmer's Mountain Vale, Julian, California

...and the Winner!

Rating	Varietal	Place of Purchase
1	**Sugar Cream**	**Puckett's, Kokomo, Indiana**

Pie Research

Plate lunches. Fried chicken. Biscuits and gravy. Chicken fried steak. Barbecue. They're out there. Just waiting. We savored them all. And came back for more. But our favorite was pie. We found ourselves eating – and enjoying – considerable helpings of it. Much more than we would have at home, that's for sure. At first we just said "Why not? We are, after all, on a trip." Then we started getting serious. We started taking notes. We started doing **Pie Research.**

All told, we probably consumed close to 60 pieces/slices/slabs of pie. Pie with lunch was a necessity. Pie for breakfast a worthy adjunct. It was great. And we didn't gain hundreds of pounds, either, which was Catherine's fear. (Then again, though, we certainly didn't lose any!).

We judged on appearance, texture, slice size. But mostly we judged – you bet – on taste.

The Best: Sugar Cream

You may recall sugar cream pie from the write-up on the Duke Restaurant (pages 34-35), Kokomo's contribution to our Top 40. Yes, Jim Duke made sugar cream "famous." But not famous enough to carry its laurels, it appears, outside of central Indiana. We loved it at first bite. And second. And third. You get the idea. What makes it so irresistibly tasty is right there in its name: it's super sweet and it's creamy rich. Try it and who knows…you may want to move to Kokomo!

Catherine's Sugar Cream Pie

1½ cups sugar
¾ cup flour
3 cups whipping cream
1½ teaspoons vanilla
dash of nutmeg

Mix all ingredients except nutmeg. Pour mixture into pie shell. Sprinkle with nutmeg. Bake for 15 minutes at 450°. Then reduce to 350° and bake for an additional 30 minutes. Refrigerate until settled and chilled. Serve. Enjoy.

Welcome to Kokomo

Sign, Route 71
North, Hosston

Barb's Cafe, Hosston, Louisiana

Barb's is part of a grocery store/package store/gas station complex that just about sums up downtown Hosston, on U.S. Highway 71, 30 miles north of Shreveport. Since Barb's is the "Home of the Wimpy" we naturally ordered a couple of them. "It's a hamburger as big as the plate. You may have wished you'd ordered just one," we were told by Barb's only other customer, Jack Green. Jack was right. They were huge. Wimpy, the Popeye comic strip character who loved hamburgers, would be proud.

Dugas Cafe, Sunset, Louisiana

The big news at the Dugas Cafe (closed the afternoon we found it; open the next morning when we returned) was filmland. Hollywood had traveled to Sunset, roughly a dozen miles north of Lafayette, to film a movie. Aristide Dugas, proprietor of the Dugas, wasn't positive as to the movie's name (he thought it was THE APOSTLE). He was positive, though, that it stars Robert Duvall. And he was positive he and his cafe are in it! "They (the film crew) closed down the restaurant for three days," reported Aristide. "But they," he quickly adds, "paid me so well I did much better than if I'd stayed open."

The cafe was built in 1948, in the days when Sunset was "The Sweet Potato Capital of the World." (The cafe's address is Yam Street and Highway 182). Aristide and his wife Ida have owned it since 1961. "For 36 years and seven months," he says with noticeable pride.

Maria and an old Corner Grill sign and a new Corner Grill sign.

Corner Grill, Lucama, North Carolina

After Louisiana it was giant steps for us. We were running behind: time to focus on our remaining targets and get Catherine (who teaches first grade in Bath, Maine) back to her classroom. The outcome was that we devoted far less time and effort to interaction with present-day cafes. There were, luckily, a few exceptions. The Corner Grill was one of them. The Corner, located on U.S. Highway 301 about 45 miles southeast of Raleigh, looks like a former Howard Johnson's. It's actually a former filling station. Nowadays it's celebrated, most of all, for its hot dogs. And waitress and "head boss" Maria McVey isn't the least bit bashful about it. "Our hot dogs are the best," she states right off. Asked what makes them so special, she answers "The red-casing hot dogs from Carolina Packers, the old-fashioned split-top buns, and the homemade (it takes eight hours to make) chili sauce. And," Maria's quick to add with a big smile, "the people who serve them."

Tipton's Cafe, Greenville, Tennessee

Tipton's isn't a diner. But it sure feels like one. It's compact: 14 stools long by ten feet wide. Everyone seems to know everyone, and to love to banter with everyone. And co-proprietor Jim Cutshaw cooks your meal – the cooked-to-order portion, anyway – right there in front of you.

Located on a side street in downtown Greenville (in the Volunteer State's eastern panhandle), Tipton's began as Linton's Cafe in 1942. Jim and his wife Edna have owned and operated it since 1973. We asked Jim (who, it should be noted, served up the finest batch of grits we enjoyed on either side of the Mason-Dixon line) how he likes the restaurant business. "Well," he replied, "I've been here 24 years, so I might as well love it." It's obvious he does.

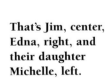

That's Jim, center, Edna, right, and their daughter Michelle, left.

Miss Worcester Diner, Worcester, Massachusetts

The Miss Worcester not only feels like a diner… it is one. To travel anywhere near Worcester – birthplace of so many, many dining cars: see page 14 – and not eat at one of its still-going-strong diners is just not right. We like the Miss Worcester because it carries on the wonderful tradition of diners having "Miss" as their first name (the reason: to add some feminine appeal to what, in days of old, was largely a male bastion). The folks at *Roadside Magazine* (located in Worcester) show 17 such diners yet with us today. The folks at the American Diner Museum (located in Providence) estimate 18. Good examples include the Miss Newport and Miss Bellows Falls, in Vermont, the Miss Adams and Miss Florence, in Massachusetts, the Miss Washington, in New Britain, Connecticut, and one of our very favorites, the Miss Portland, in Maine. You can't miss (Sorry!) with any of them.

The Nicest Highlight

During our voyage we, via postcards and telephone, kept the folks back home aware of at least some of our doings. They, in turn, hit the highlights for us. Selecting the nicest highlight was a shoo-in when Catherine's sister, Patricia, shared with us the news that Maine's oldest diner, the Palace, was going to be re-opening. That was exciting. So much so that, on the very last day of our Trip of a Lifetime, we swung by and took a photo. It felt good. Please turn the page to see why.

Palace Diner,
Biddeford, Maine
August 22, 1997

For More

Come on in and join the
fun. The sign said it all on
Grand Re-Opening Day,
October 20, 1997.

Palace Diner, Biddeford, Maine

What better way to end WHERE HAVE YOU GONE, STARLIGHT CAFE? than with a
success story? And the Palace *is* a success story.

Built by a long-defunct small diner manufacturing firm – Pollard & Co., of Lowell,
Massachusetts – the Palace arrived in Biddeford (located 15 miles south of Portland on
U.S. Route 1) in 1927, the year the Babe belted his 60 and "Lucky Lindy" hopped the
Atlantic. Legend has it that it was called the "Palace" because someone at the factory in
Lowell remarked "Gee whiz, that looks just like a little palace."

The Palace had but three proprietors in the years between 1927 and June 1996. It
was then closed, and sat vacant until the summer of '97 when it was purchased by the
husband and wife team of Rick and Jo Bernier. The Berniers, with the help of a lot of
friends (Rick: "It was like a team effort."), revitalized the 70-year-old diner. The Grand
Re-Opening was October 20th. And it *was* grand. For Rick it was the culmination of a
long-standing dream. "It's what I've been wanting," he beams. "It feels like the diner has
its heart beating again."

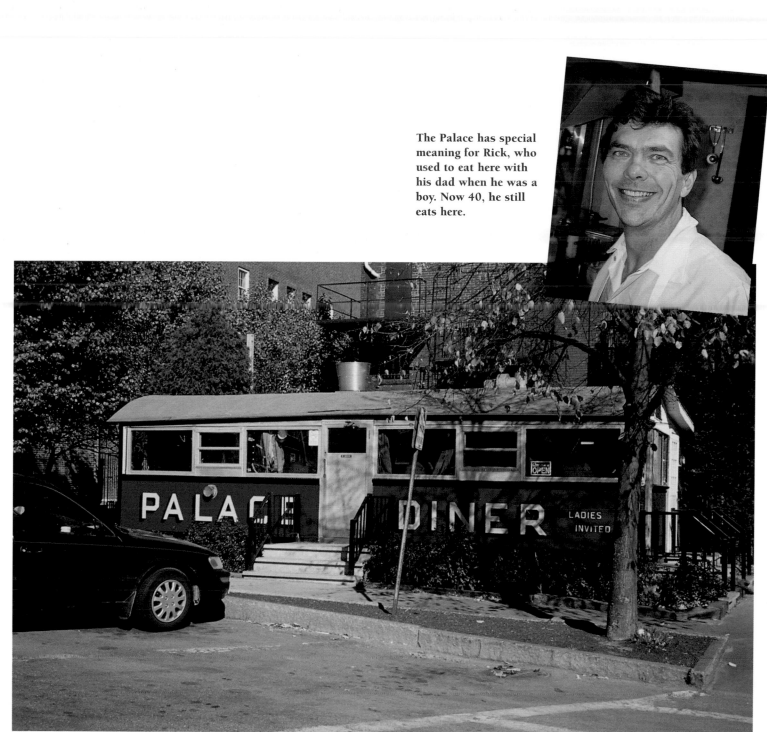

The Palace has special meaning for Rick, who used to eat here with his dad when he was a boy. Now 40, he still eats here.

"…just like a little palace."

Index